# Programming for Problem Solving - II

## THE AUTHORS

**Dr. Shakti Kumar** is currently working as Director, Panipat Institute of Engineering and Technology, Panipat. He is having more than 32 years of experience in Teaching, Research and Administration He Served as a Founder Vice Chancellor, SDGI Global University, Ghaziabad, Uttar Pradesh and Vice Chancellor, Baddi University of Emerging Sciences & Technology, Baddi, Distt. Solan, Himachal Pradesh.

**Dr. Shakti Arora** is a renowned academician and cybersecurity expert, currently heading the B.Tech. CSE Department at Panipat Institute of Engineering & Technology (PIET). With over 19 years of experience, she specializes in blockchain, cybersecurity, and AI. She has published extensively in reputed journals and conferences. As a mentor, she has led students in national hackathons and start-ups initiatives. She is recognized as an advanced level Innovation Ambassador; Dr. Arora is dedicated to advancing technology education and fostering innovation among aspiring engineers and entrepreneurs

**Ms. Shreya Sharma**, is presently working in PIET, Samalkha. She is pursuing Ph.D from MMU Mullana, Ambala. She is a passionate educator and researcher with a strong background in computer science and actively engages in AI and data science. She excels in teaching and research, publishing in top journals like IEEE.

**Mr. Anil Kumar Tanwar** a distinguished Engineering professional with over 15 years of experience in R&D, Manufacturing Process, and Quality Engineering. Multi-disciplinary specialization in Vacuum Technologies, High-Frequency THz devices, with research interests extend to IoT, Smart devices and dedicated to advancing innovation in R&D. Anil holds a Bachelor's degree in Electronics & Communications Engineering from Sabarmati University, Gujarat, India.

**Dr. B.K. Verma** is Working as Professor and Head of the Department in CSE- Artificial Intelligence and Data Science, Panipat Institute of Engineering and Technology (PIET), Haryana. He is having 18 Years Experience in Academic, Research and Administrative. He Published 52 Research Articles in SCI/SCOPUS/WOS and 32 Patent in National and International.

# Programming for Problem Solving - II

*Authors*
**Dr. Shakti Kumar**
**Dr. Shakti Arora**
**Ms Shreya Sharma**
**Mr. Anil Tanwar**
**Dr. BK Verma**

ACADEMIC ENCLAVE

*First Edition, 2025*

ISBN: 978-93-48642-89-9

*Published by*
**ACADEMIC ENCLAVE**
House No. 10/15, Ground Floor,
Block-A, Street No. 14/3, Kamal Vihar,
Kamal Pur, Burari, Delhi-110084
*Email: info@academicenclave.com*
*Phone: 011-45502728 Mobile: +91-7042423166*
*Website: www.academicenclave.com*

# Preface

This book is designed to provide an in-depth exploration of key concepts that empower learners to develop advanced problem-solving skills using Python. The book builds on fundamental Python knowledge and progresses to more complex topics, including data structures, functions, error handling, and data analysis. Each chapter is structured to introduce theoretical concepts, followed by practical examples and exercises that reinforce learning and encourage hands-on practice. By the end of the book, readers will have developed the skills required to write efficient, error-free code and perform data analysis with Python, equipping them for real-world programming challenges. The book covers a wide range of topics, starting with the basics of Python fundamentals, such as variables, operators, and control flow, before diving into essential data structures like lists, tuples, dictionaries, and sets. It also emphasizes the importance of functions and error handling to write modular and robust code. The final section focuses on Python's powerful capabilities for data analysis, using libraries such as NumPy, Pandas, and Matplotlib. Through clear explanations and engaging examples, this book prepares readers to solve problems effectively and apply Python to a variety of fields, including software development and data science.

**Dr. Shakti Kumar**

**Dr. Shakti Arora**

**Ms Shreya Sharma**

**Mr. Anil Tanwar**

**Dr. BK Verma**

# Contents

CHAPTER - 1

# Python Fundamentals, Basic Data Types & Operators

## Overview of Python

Python is a versatile and user-friendly programming language known for its readability, simplicity, and powerful capabilities across various domains. Created in the early 1990s by Guido van Rossum, Python has grown into one of the most popular programming languages, favored by both beginners and seasoned developers. Its syntax is designed to be easy to understand, closely resembling English, which makes it particularly appealing to those new to programming. Python's high-level, interpreted nature means code is executed line-by-line, which facilitates testing and debugging, making the development process smoother and more intuitive. Python's adaptability lies in its support for multiple programming paradigms, including procedural, object-oriented, and functional programming. This versatility allows it to be used across different kinds of projects, from simple scripting to building complex applications. The language's dynamically typed nature further adds to its flexibility, enabling developers to create adaptable and concise code without the need to declare variable types explicitly. Additionally, Python's extensive standard library, along with a vast ecosystem of third-party packages, provides pre-built functions for a wide range of applications, saving time and effort for developers by reducing the need for repetitive coding tasks.

Python has a strong foothold in many fields, including data science, web development, artificial intelligence, and scientific computing. For data scientists and machine learning engineers, Python offers libraries like NumPy, Pandas, and TensorFlow, which simplify data manipulation, statistical analysis, and model building. In web development, frameworks like Django and Flask allow developers to create robust and scalable web applications. Python's compatibility with IoT and embedded systems has also made it popular for scripting and automation, enabling applications in everything from data entry automation to device control in smart homes.The language's future looks promising as it continues to evolve, backed by the Python Software Foundation and a large, active community that constantly contributes improvements, tutorials, and resources. While Python may not always be the best fit for performance-critical applications due to its slower speed compared to compiled languages, its accessibility and wide application scope make it an invaluable tool. As demand for fields like AI and data science grows, Python's role as a foundational programming language is only expected to strengthen, ensuring its relevance and adaptability in an ever-evolving technological landscape.

## History of Python and its Importance

The history of Python begins in the late 1980s, when Dutch programmer Guido van Rossum sought to develop a new language that combined the ease of scripting with the power of more complex programming languages. While working at Centrum Wiskunde & Informatica (CWI) in the Netherlands, Van Rossum aimed to create a language that was accessible, easy to read, and versatile enough for a range of tasks, from simple scripts to sophisticated software systems. Python was conceived as a successor to the ABC programming language, which Van Rossum had worked on previously. ABC was intended to be a beginner-friendly language, but it had limitations in extensibility and flexibility. Python was envisioned as a way to retain ABC's simplicity while enhancing its functionality to meet a broader range of programming needs.

The language was officially born in December 1989, when Van Rossum began writing Python during the Christmas holidays. He chose the name "Python" not after the snake but as a nod to the British comedy group Monty Python, whose surreal sense of humor influenced Van Rossum's vision for the language as something fun and approachable. Python's first official release, Python 0.9.0, came in February 1991. This initial version included several core features that remain central to Python today, such as exception handling, functions, and classes. Van Rossum also implemented Python with an interactive shell, which allowed users to test code line by line—a feature that contributed significantly to its popularity among programmers.

Python 1.0 was released in January 1994, marking its first official stable release. This version introduced important features like lambda, map, filter, and reduce functions, which reflected Python's support for functional programming paradigms alongside object-oriented and procedural approaches. The language gained a steady following throughout the 1990s, especially among academic and scientific communities, who appreciated Python's simplicity and ease of integration with other languages like C and C++. As the internet grew in the late 1990s, Python's popularity surged due to the introduction of web frameworks like Zope, which allowed developers to use Python in web development. By this time, the language was managed by the Python Software Foundation (PSF), a nonprofit organization that oversees the development and promotion of Python.

The release of Python 2.0 in October 2000 was a significant milestone, introducing features like list comprehensions, garbage collection, and the new Unicode support, which broadened Python's international usability. However, it was the launch of Python 3.0 in December 2008 that marked the most substantial evolution in Python's history. Python 3 introduced backward-incompatible changes to clean up Python's syntax and streamline its functionality, making it more efficient and modern but also creating a challenge for developers who had to migrate code from Python 2 to Python 3. Over the next decade, Python 3 became the standard as Python 2 was officially deprecated in 2020. Python has since continued to evolve, with regular updates adding new features and performance improvements while maintaining its core philosophy of simplicity, readability, and flexibility. Today, Python's vibrant community and extensive library ecosystem have made it one of the most popular programming languages, widely used across fields from web development to artificial intelligence.

**Table 1.1: Milestones in Python's History.**

| Year | Version | Milestone/Feature | Description |
|---|---|---|---|
| 1989 | Development | Guido van Rossum starts Python development | Began during the Christmas holidays at CWI, Netherlands as a successor to the ABC language. |
| 1991 | Python 0.9.0 | First public release | Included core features: exception handling, functions, and classes, along with an interactive shell. |
| 1994 | Python 1.0 | Official first stable release | Introduced features like lambda, map, filter, and reduce, supporting functional programming. |
| Late 1990s | - | Rise in popularity for web development | Frameworks like Zope helped Python gain traction in the web development community. |
| 2000 | Python 2.0 | Major update introducing list comprehensions and garbage collection | Released by the Python Software Foundation, it added new features like Unicode support and list comprehensions. |
| 2001 | - | Establishment of the Python Software Foundation (PSF) | Nonprofit organization formed to support and manage the development of Python. |
| 2008 | Python 3.0 | Introduction of backward-incompatible changes for modern improvements | Major overhaul with simplified syntax, performance improvements, and modernized features. |
| 2010s | Python 3.x | Incremental improvements | Regular updates, including performance boosts, improved libraries, and type hinting, were made to establish Python 3 as a standard. |
| 2020 | End of Python 2 | Python 2 officially deprecated | Python 2 is discontinued, encouraging migration to Python 3 for all users. |

| Year | Version | Milestone/Feature | Description |
|---|---|---|---|
| Present | Ongoing | Continuous development of Python 3.x versions | Ongoing updates focus on speed, security, and expanding the standard library, keeping Python at the forefront of programming. |

This Table 1.1 highlights the key developments that have shaped Python into the popular language it is today.

## Importance of Python

Python holds significant importance in the programming world for several reasons. Its simplicity, versatility, and wide-ranging applications make it a foundational tool across various fields, from web development to data science, artificial intelligence, automation, and beyond (Figure 1.1.).

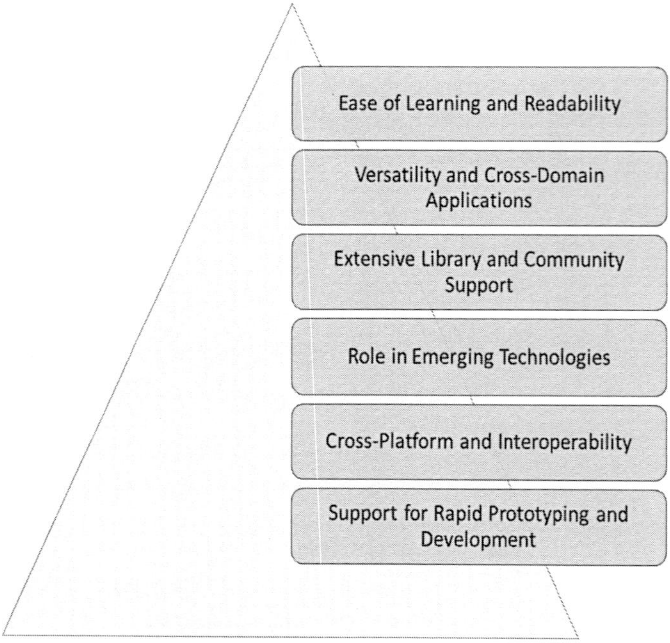


**Figure 1.1: Importance of Python**

*Here's why Python is particularly important:*

## 1. Ease of Learning and Readability

Python's simple and readable syntax makes it one of the most beginner-friendly languages, allowing new programmers to focus on core programming concepts without being overwhelmed by complex syntax rules. Python code closely resembles English, which lowers the barrier to entry and enables programmers to learn faster and write code that is easy to understand and maintain. This accessibility is a significant reason why Python is commonly used in education, especially for introducing programming in schools and universities.

## 2. Versatility and Cross-Domain Applications

Python's ability to support multiple programming paradigms, including procedural, object-oriented, and functional programming, makes it a highly versatile language. This versatility is supported by Python's extensive libraries and frameworks, which enable its use across a wide range of industries and applications:

- Data Science and Machine Learning: Python is the leading language in data science, thanks to libraries like Pandas, NumPy, and Matplotlib for data manipulation and visualization, and TensorFlow, Scikit-learn, and PyTorch for machine learning.
- Web Development: Frameworks like Django and Flask make Python a popular choice for developing secure, scalable, and fast web applications.
- Automation and Scripting: Python is used to automate repetitive tasks, making it valuable in IT operations, testing, and data processing.
- Scientific Computing: Libraries like SciPy make Python indispensable in research, engineering, and scientific computing.

## 3. Extensive Library and Community Support

Python's rich ecosystem includes a vast standard library and an even larger collection of third-party packages. This enables developers to access pre-built functionality for almost any task, reducing the need for complex coding from scratch. The Python Package Index (PyPI) hosts thousands of packages for various needs, from data processing to web scraping, making Python highly adaptable for new applications and innovations. Also, Python's active community provides extensive documentation, tutorials, forums, and tools, making it easy to find help and resources for any programming challenge.

## 4. Role in Emerging Technologies

Python is at the forefront of emerging technologies such as artificial intelligence (AI), machine learning (ML), and deep learning. Its frameworks, such as TensorFlow, Keras, and PyTorch, are widely used for building and deploying AI models. Python's flexibility and performance make it ideal for rapid prototyping and experimentation in these fields, where fast iteration is essential. Additionally, Python's compatibility with other languages and tools allows developers to integrate Python-based solutions with IoT devices, robotics, and blockchain technology, placing it at the heart of innovation in cutting-edge technology sectors.

## 5. Cross-Platform and Interoperability

Python is cross-platform, meaning it can run on various operating systems, including Windows, macOS, and Linux, with minimal changes to the code. This makes Python ideal for collaborative projects where different team members might use different systems. Python also offers interoperability with other programming languages, such as C/C++, Java, and R, enabling developers to combine Python with performance-oriented languages where needed. This cross-platform capability enhances Python's appeal in industries where applications need to be flexible and compatible with diverse systems.

## 6. Support for Rapid Prototyping and Development

Python's interpreted nature and dynamically typed approach make it especially suitable for rapid development cycles. Developers can write and test Python code in real-time, making it easier to develop and iterate quickly, which is crucial in today's fast-paced tech landscape. Python's adaptability and ease of prototyping make it ideal for startups and research teams who need to move quickly from concept to product.

# Python Installation

Installing Python is a straightforward process, and it can be done on various operating systems, including Windows, macOS, and Linux. Here's a detailed guide on how to install Python on each of these platforms (Table 1.2).

**Table 1.2:Steps to install Python on Different Operating Systems.**

| Step | Instructions |
|---|---|
| 1. Download Python | Go to python.org, click "Downloads," and select the latest Python version for your operating system (Windows, macOS, or Linux). |
| 2. Run the Installer | Open the downloaded file and follow the installation prompts. For Windows users, check "Add Python to PATH" before clicking "Install Now" to simplify access. |
| 3. Verify Installation | Open the Command Prompt (Windows) or Terminal (macOS/Linux) and type python --version or python3 --version to confirm Python is installed correctly. |
| 4. Install pip (optional) | Type pip --version in Command Prompt or Terminal to check if pip is installed. If not, install it by following your system's instructions (Linux users may need sudo apt install python3-pip). |

## 1. Installing Python on Windows

### i. Download the Installer:

Go to the official Python website and click on the "Downloads" section.

The website should automatically detect your operating system and suggest the latest stable version of Python. Click the download link for Windows.

### ii. Run the Installer:

- Open the downloaded .exe file. A Python installer window will appear.
- **Important**: Check the box that says "Add Python to PATH." This ensures that you can run Python from the command line without specifying its directory.
- Choose "Install Now" to install Python with default settings, or select "Customize Installation" if you want to modify settings (e.g., choose the installation location or install optional features).

### iii. Verify the Installation:

- Open the Command Prompt by typing cmd in the Windows search bar and running the application.
- Type python --version or python to check if Python is installed correctly. You should see the Python version you installed.

## 2. Installing Python on macOS

### i. Download the Installer:

- Visit the Python website and go to the "Downloads" section.
- Select the latest version of Python for macOS.

### ii. Run the Installer:

- Open the downloaded .pkg file. The Python installer will guide you through the installation steps.
- Follow the instructions and confirm any required settings to complete the installation.

### iii. Verify the Installation:

- Open the Terminal application (you can find it in Applications > Utilities or by searching "Terminal" in Spotlight).
- Type python3 --version to confirm the installation. (On macOS, Python 3 is typically referred to as python3 because some versions of macOS come with Python 2 pre-installed as python.)

## 3. Installing Python on Linux

Python is often pre-installed on many Linux distributions, especially Python 2.x versions. However, you may need to install Python 3.x or upgrade to the latest version.

### i. Check Existing Installation:

- Open a terminal window and type python3 --version. If Python 3 is already installed, the version number will display.
- If Python 3 is not installed or you need to upgrade, proceed with the steps below.

### ii. Install Python 3 Using the Package Manager:

- Use the appropriate package manager for your distribution to install Python:
- **Ubuntu/Debian**: Run sudo apt update followed by sudo apt install python3.
- **Fedora**: Run sudo dnf install python3.
- **Arch Linux**: Run sudo pacman -S python.

### iii. Verify the Installation:

- After installation, type python3 --version in the terminal to check the installed version.

## 4. Installing Additional Tools

Once Python is installed, it's a good idea to install **pip**, Python's package manager, if it hasn't already been installed automatically. With pip, you can easily install additional packages and libraries.

- **On Windows and macOS**: Pip is typically installed along with Python. Check by typing pip --version in the terminal or command prompt.
- **On Linux**: If pip is not installed, use the command sudo apt install python3-pip for Debian/Ubuntu or sudo dnf install python3-pip for Fedora.

## 5. Using a Virtual Environment (Optional)

A virtual environment is a tool to keep dependencies required by different projects in separate places. You can create a virtual environment with:

```
python3 -m venv myenv
```

This creates an isolated environment named myenv in your current directory. You can activate it with:

- **Windows**: myenv\Scripts\activate
- **macOS/Linux**: source myenv/bin/activate

After installing Python, you'll be ready to start developing by accessing Python directly from the terminal or command prompt. You can also install an integrated development environment (IDE) like **PyCharm**, **VS Code**, or **Jupyter Notebook** for a more advanced coding experience.

## Variables

In Python, variables are essential building blocks used to store, reference, and manipulate data throughout your program. Variables are like containers that hold values, allowing you to use and manipulate those values in different parts of the code.

### 1. Declaring Variables

In Python, you don't need to explicitly declare the type of a variable. Instead, you just assign a value to a variable name, and Python automatically infers its type. This is because Python is a dynamically-typed language.

You simply use the = operator to assign a value:

```
# Example of variable assignment
name = "Alice" # A string variable
age = 25         # An integer variable
height = 5.8     # A float variable
is_student = True     # A boolean variable1.
```

In the example above:

- name holds a string value "Alice".
- age holds an integer 25.
- height holds a floating-point number 5.8.
- is_student holds a boolean value True.

### 2. Variable Naming Rules and Conventions

Python has specific rules and conventions for naming variables:

- Variable names must start with a letter (a-z, A-Z) or an underscore _, but cannot start with a number.
- The name can contain letters, numbers, and underscores but no special characters (e.g., @, -, %).
- Python is case-sensitive, so age and Age would be two different variables.
- Descriptive variable names are encouraged for readability, e.g., user_age or total_price.

***Examples:***

```
# Valid variable names
first_name = "John"
user_age = 30
_is_verified = True
```

```
# Invalid variable names
1name = "Alice"      # Starts with a number
user-age = 25        # Contains a hyphen
total$price = 100    # Contains a special character
```

## 3. Variable Types in Python

Python supports various data types, which are automatically assigned based on the value given. Common data types include:

- Integer (int): Whole numbers, e.g., 10, -5.
- Float (float): Decimal numbers, e.g., 3.14, -0.5.
- String (str): Text enclosed in quotes, e.g., "Hello", 'World'.
- Boolean (bool): Logical values True or False.
- List: Ordered, mutable collection of items, e.g., [1, 2, 3].
- Tuple: Ordered, immutable collection, e.g., (1, 2, 3).
- Dictionary (dict): Collection of key-value pairs, e.g., {'name': 'Alice', 'age': 25}.

***Example of using multiple types:***

```
# Different data types in variables
count = 10                     # Integer
price = 19.99                  # Float
name = "Notebook"              # String
is_available = True            # Boolean
features = ["Pages", "Cover"] # List
dimensions = (8.5, 11)         # Tuple
product_info = {'name': 'Notebook', 'price': 19.99} #
Dictionary
```

### 4. Changing Variable Values

In Python, variables are mutable, which means you can change the value of a variable after it is assigned:

```
# Changing the value of a variable
age = 30
print(age)    # Output: 30

age = 35
print(age)    # Output: 35
```

Python also allows you to change the type of data held by a variable, as Python does not enforce a fixed type for a variable:

```
value = 10          # Integer
print(type(value)) # Output: <class 'int'>

value = "Ten"       # String
print(type(value)) # Output: <class 'str'>
```

### 5. Scope of Variables

Variables in Python have scope, which determines where they can be accessed:

- Global Variables: Defined outside of functions, accessible throughout the program.
- Local Variables: Defined inside functions, accessible only within that function.

***Example:***

```
x = "global variable"  # Global variable
def my_function():
    y = "local variable"  # Local variable
    print(y)

print(x)       # Output: global variable
my_function()  # Output: local variable
print(y)       # Error, y is not accessible outside the
function
```

### 6. Constants

While Python does not have a built-in constant type, a common convention is to use all uppercase letters to indicate a variable that should not change, e.g., PI = 3.14159. However, this is by convention only, and Python does not prevent reassignment of these values.

```
PI = 3.14159
GRAVITY = 9.8
```

### 7. Best Practices for Variables

- Use descriptive names (e.g., user_name, total_price).
- Avoid using single letters like x, y, unless used in loops or temporary calculations.
- Follow the naming conventions and keep variable names consistent.
- Avoid reusing variable names with different types in the same scope, as it can lead to confusion.

Understanding variables is essential for effective programming in Python. Proper use of variables and their types can help in writing clear, organized, and efficient code.

## Constants

In Python, constants are variables that are intended to have a fixed value throughout the execution of a program. While Python does not have a built-in mechanism to enforce immutability (i.e., to prevent changes to a variable after it's been set), developers use naming conventions and external tools to indicate and handle constants. Here's a deeper look at how constants are handled in Python:

### 1. Defining Constants in Python

Python developers typically use all uppercase letters to define a constant. This naming convention signals to others that the variable is intended to be a constant and should not be changed. However, unlike some other programming languages, Python won't prevent you from reassigning a new value to a constant—so the immutability is by convention only.

***Example:***

```
PI = 3.14159
GRAVITY = 9.8
SPEED_OF_LIGHT = 299792458  # meters per second
```

### i. In the example above:

- PI, GRAVITY, and SPEED_OF_LIGHT are intended to remain unchanged throughout the program.
- By using uppercase letters, you indicate that these values are constants and should not be modified.

### 2. Using Constants in Modules

One common practice in larger Python projects is to place constants in a separate file, usually named something like constants.py. By doing so, you can import these constants into other files or modules, making it easier to manage and update them in one place.

***Example of a constants.py file:***

```
# constants.py
PI = 3.14159
EULER_NUMBER = 2.71828
AVOGADRO_CONSTANT = 6.02214076e23
```

You can then use these constants in other parts of your project:

```
# main.py
import constants

print(constants.PI)
print(constants.EULER_NUMBER)
```

### 3. Avoiding Accidental Modification of Constants

Since Python does not enforce immutability, it's possible to accidentally reassign a constant. To prevent this, follow these best practices:

- Naming Conventions: Use uppercase letters for constants to remind developers not to modify them.
- Documentation: Clearly document which variables are constants.
- External Libraries: Use libraries like mypy or pylint to perform static checks on your code. These tools can catch accidental modifications to constants, especially when paired with type hints and strict type checking.

### 4. Using enum for Constant-Like Behavior

For a fixed set of constants, you can use the enum module, which allows you to define a set of related constants and gives each a unique value. Enums are helpful when you have a group of related constants that should not change, such as specific statuses or categories.

***Example:***

```
from enum import Enum
class Status(Enum):
    NEW = 1
    IN_PROGRESS = 2
    COMPLETED = 3
print(Status.NEW)          # Output: Status.NEW
print(Status.NEW.value)    # Output: 1
```

In this example, Status is an enumeration with predefined values that represent different statuses. Unlike regular constants, the enum values are somewhat more protected, making them less prone to modification.

### 5. Using frozen dataclasses for Constant Collections

If you need a collection of constants, such as a set of related configuration values, you can use a @dataclass with frozen=True to create an immutable dataclass. This will raise an error if you attempt to change the values after creation.

***Example:***

```
from dataclasses import dataclass
@dataclass(frozen=True)
class AppConfig:
    API_URL: str = "https://api.example.com"
    MAX_CONNECTIONS: int = 5
    TIMEOUT: int = 100

config = AppConfig()
# config.API_URL = "https://newapi.example.com"
# This will raise an error
```

In this example, AppConfig is a frozen dataclass, and attempting to modify any attribute will raise an error, ensuring immutability for this set of constants.

## Identifiers

Identifiers in Python are names given to entities such as variables, functions, classes, and modules. They are fundamental in programming as they allow you to refer to these entities in your code, facilitating clear and organized communication with the programming language. Here's a detailed exploration of identifiers in Python:

### 1. Definition of Identifiers

An identifier is a name used to identify a variable, function, class, module, or other object in a Python program. Identifiers can consist of letters, digits, and underscores, but they must adhere to specific rules and conventions.

### 2. Rules for Naming Identifiers

To create valid identifiers in Python, you must follow these rules:

#### i. Allowed Characters: Identifiers can contain:

- Letters (both uppercase A-Z and lowercase a-z)
- Digits (0-9), but they cannot start with a digit
- Underscores (_)

#### ii. Starting Character: An identifier must start with:

- A letter (A-Z or a-z) or
- An underscore (_)

**Case Sensitivity**: Identifiers are case-sensitive. This means that variable, Variable, and VARIABLE are considered three distinct identifiers.

**No Special Characters**: Identifiers cannot include special characters such as @, $, %, -, etc.

**Reserved Keywords**: Python has reserved keywords that cannot be used as identifiers because they have special meanings in the language. Examples include if, for, while, def, class, and others.

***Examples of valid and invalid identifiers:***

```
# Valid identifiers
name = "Alice"
age = 30
employee_ID = 12345
total_price = 99.99

# Invalid identifiers
1st_name = "Bob"        # Starts with a digit
user-age = 25           # Contains a hyphen
total$price = 100.0     # Contains a special character
class = "data"          # 'class' is a reserved keyword
```

## 3. Naming Conventions for Identifiers

While Python allows a wide range of names for identifiers, adhering to naming conventions improves code readability and maintainability. Some common conventions include:

- **Variable and Function Names**: Use snake_case for naming, where words are separated by underscores.

***For example:***

```
total_price = 100.0
def calculate_sum(a, b):
  return a + b
```

- **Constant Names**: Use all uppercase letters with words separated by underscores to indicate that the value should not change:

```
PI = 3.14159
MAX_CONNECTIONS = 10
```

- **Class Names**: Use PascalCase (also known as CamelCase), where each word starts with an uppercase letter:

```
class DataManager:
    pass
```

- **Private Variables**: Use a single leading underscore (_) to indicate that a variable is intended for internal use:

```
_internal_variable = "private"
```

- **Strongly Private Variables**: Use two leading underscores (__) for variables to invoke name mangling, making it harder to create subclasses that accidentally override the private attributes and methods:

```
class SampleClass:
    def __init__(self):
        self.__private_var = "private"
```

## 4. Scope of Identifiers

The scope of an identifier determines its visibility and lifespan within a program. In Python, identifiers can have different scopes:

- **Local Scope**: Identifiers defined within a function or a block are considered local. They are only accessible within that function or block.

```
def my_function():
    local_variable = 10  # Local scope
    print(local_variable)


my_function()  # Output: 10
# print(local_variable)  # Raises NameError, as it's not
accessible here
```

- **Global Scope**: Identifiers defined at the top level of a script or module are global. They are accessible throughout the module and can be accessed inside functions unless shadowed by a local identifier.

```
global_variable = 20  # Global scope


def my_function():
    print(global_variable)  # Accessible here


my_function()  # Output: 20
```

- **Built-in Scope**: Python has a set of built-in identifiers that are always available. These include functions like print() and len(), as well as exceptions and constants.

## Comments

Comments in Python are annotations in the code that are not executed as part of the program. They serve as explanatory notes for anyone reading the code, providing context, descriptions, and clarifications. Comments are essential for improving code readability, maintaining it over time, and facilitating collaboration among developers. Here's a detailed overview of comments in Python:

### 1. Types of Comments

Python supports two main types of comments:

### a. Single-Line Comments

Single-line comments are created by placing a hash symbol (#) before the comment text. Everything on the line after the # is considered a comment and is ignored by the Python interpreter.

*Example:*

```
# This is a single-line comment
x = 10  # This comment explains that x is assigned the value 10
```

### b. Multi-Line Comments

While Python does not have a specific multi-line comment syntax, multi-line comments can be effectively created using triple quotes (''' or """). Although this is often used for docstrings (a type of comment that documents functions, classes, or modules), it can also serve as a way to comment out blocks of code.

*Example:*

```
'''
This is a multi-line comment.
It can span multiple lines.
'''
y = 20  # This assigns 20 to y
```

### 2. Docstrings

Docstrings are a specific type of comment used to document Python modules, classes, methods, and functions. They are defined using triple quotes and can be accessed through the __doc__ attribute. Docstrings should be used to describe what a function or class does, its parameters, return values, and any exceptions it may raise.

*Example:*

```
def add(a, b):
    """
    Add two numbers together.
    Parameters:
    a (int or float): The first number.
    b (int or float): The second number.
    Returns:
    int or float: The sum of a and b.
    """
    return a + b
print(add.__doc__)  # Outputs the docstring of the add function
```

### 3. Best Practices for Using Comments

Using comments effectively requires a thoughtful approach. Here are some best practices:

- Be Clear and Concise: Comments should be straightforward and to the point. Avoid unnecessary verbosity; instead, focus on clarity.
- Explain Why, Not What: While comments can explain what the code does, it's often more useful to explain why certain decisions were made. The code itself should be clear enough to describe what it does.
- Update Comments: As code evolves, make sure to update comments to reflect any changes. Outdated comments can be misleading and confusing.
- Avoid Obvious Comments: Comments should add value. Avoid stating the obvious, such as # Increment x by 1 before x += 1, which is self-explanatory.
- Use Docstrings for Documentation: Utilize docstrings to provide comprehensive documentation for functions, classes, and modules. This is particularly helpful for users of your code who need to understand how to use your functions without delving into the implementation details.

### 4. When to Use Comments

Comments should be used in the following situations:

- Complex Logic: When the logic of a piece of code is complex or non-intuitive, add comments to clarify what is happening and why.
- Important Decisions: If a particular choice in your code is critical or unconventional, explain the reasoning behind it.
- To Do Notes: Use comments to mark sections of code that require further work or investigation.

*For example:*

```
# TODO: Refactor this function to improve performance
```

Comments are an essential part of writing maintainable and understandable Python code. By using single-line comments, multi-line comments, and docstrings effectively, you can provide valuable context to your code. Following best practices for commenting will enhance the clarity of your code and facilitate easier collaboration with other developers.

## Reserved Keywords

Reserved keywords in Python are special words that have predefined meanings in the language and cannot be used as identifiers (names for variables, functions, classes, etc.). These keywords define the syntax and structure of Python code, enabling the interpreter to understand how to execute the program. Understanding reserved keywords is essential for writing correct and efficient Python code.

### List of Reserved Keywords

As of Python 3.x, the following are the reserved keywords (Table 1.3)

**Table 1.3: Reserved Keywords**

| Keyword | Description |
|---|---|
| False | Boolean value representing false. |
| None | Represents the absence of a value or a null value. |
| True | Boolean value representing true. |
| and | Logical operator that returns True if both operands are true. |
| as | Used to create an alias while importing modules. |
| assert | Used for debugging purposes; tests if a condition is true. |
| async | Used to define an asynchronous function. |
| await | Used to call an asynchronous function and wait for its result. |
| break | Exits from the nearest enclosing loop. |
| class | Used to define a new class. |
| continue | Skips the current iteration of the nearest enclosing loop and proceeds to the next iteration. |
| def | Used to define a new function. |

| | |
|---|---|
| del | Deletes an object. |
| elif | Used in conditional statements; shorthand for "else if." |
| else | Used in conditional statements; executes a block of code if the condition is false. |
| except | Used to handle exceptions; specifies a block of code to execute in case of an error. |
| finally | Defines a block of code that will be executed regardless of whether an exception occurs. |
| for | Used to create a for loop. |
| from | Used to import specific parts of a module. |
| global | Declares a variable as global, allowing it to be accessed across different functions. |
| if | Starts a conditional statement. |
| import | Imports a module or specific attributes from a module. |
| in | Used to check if a value exists within an iterable. |
| is | Tests for object identity; returns True if two references point to the same object. |
| lambda | Creates an anonymous function (a function without a name). |
| nonlocal | Declares a variable in a nested function to be non-local, allowing access to variables in the nearest enclosing scope. |
| not | Logical operator that negates a boolean value. |
| or | Logical operator that returns True if at least one of the operands is true. |
| pass | A null statement; serves as a placeholder for future code. |
| raise | Raises an exception. |
| return | Exits a function and optionally passes an expression back to the caller. |
| try | Starts a block of code that will be tested for exceptions. |
| while | Starts a while loop. |
| with | Used to wrap the execution of a block with methods defined by a context manager. |
| yield | Used in generators to return a value and suspend the function's execution, allowing it to be resumed later. |

## Characteristics of Reserved Keywords

Fixed Meaning: Each reserved keyword has a specific meaning and function in the Python programming language, which cannot be changed or redefined.

Not Usable as Identifiers: Since they are reserved for their specific purposes, you cannot use them as names for variables, functions, classes, or any other identifiers. Attempting to do so will result in a SyntaxError.

Accessing the List: You can access the list of reserved keywords programmatically using the keyword module:

```
import keyword
print(keyword.kwlist)
```

## Importance of Reserved Keywords

Structure and Flow Control: Reserved keywords help define the structure and control the flow of Python programs. They enable conditional statements, loops, function definitions, exception handling, and more.

Readability and Clarity: By using reserved keywords, Python code becomes more readable and self-explanatory. Keywords clearly indicate the purpose and action of code blocks, enhancing the overall clarity of the program.

**Prevent Errors:** Understanding and adhering to the reserved keywords prevents naming conflicts and reduces the likelihood of syntax errors in code.

## Basic Data Types

Python supports a variety of data types, which are classified into several basic categories. Each data type serves a specific purpose and is used to store different kinds of data. Python provides a rich variety of data types, including numeric types, strings, booleans, lists, tuples, dictionaries, sets, and literals. Each type has its own characteristics and use cases, allowing developers to choose the appropriate type based on the needs of their application. Understanding these data types is crucial for writing efficient and effective Python code.

Here's a detailed overview of various fundamental data types in Python, including numeric types, strings, booleans, lists, tuples, dictionaries, sets, and literals.

### 1. Numeric Types

Numeric types represent numbers in Python. There are three main numeric types:

#### *a. Integer (int)*

- Whole numbers without a decimal point, which can be positive or negative.
- Can be of arbitrary size, limited by memory rather than a fixed number of bytes.

***Example:***

```
a = 10# Positive integer
b = -5# Negative integer
c = 0# Zero
```

### *b. Float (float)*

- Represents real numbers, which include decimal points or numbers in exponential notation.
- Used for precise calculations, such as in scientific computations.

***Example:***

```
x = 3.14# A floating-point number
y = -0.001# A negative float
z = 1.5e2# Scientific notation (1.5 * 10^2 = 150.0)
```

### *c. Complex (complex)*

- Represents complex numbers in the form a + bj, where a is the real part and b is the imaginary part.
- Useful in advanced mathematical applications.

***Example:***

```
c1 = 2 + 3j# A complex number
c2 = 1 - 4j# Another complex number
```

## 2. String

Strings in Python are sequences of characters enclosed in quotes (single, double, or triple). They are immutable, meaning once created, their content cannot be changed.

***Example:***

```
str1 = "Hello, World!"# A string in double quotes
str2 = 'Python is fun!'# A string in single quotes
str3 = '''This is a
multi-line string'''# A multi-line string using triple quotes
```

## 3. Boolean

Boolean types represent truth values and can be either True or False. They are often used in conditional statements and logical operations.

***Example:***

```
is_active = True# A boolean value representing true
is_valid = False# A boolean value representing false
```

## 4. List

Lists are ordered, mutable collections of items that can contain mixed data types. Lists are defined using square brackets (`[]`) and can be modified after their creation (items can be added, removed, or changed).

***Example:***

```
fruits = ['apple', 'banana', 'cherry']  # A list of strings
numbers = [1, 2, 3.5, 4]      # A list with mixed types
```

## 5. Tuple

Tuples are similar to lists, but they are immutable, meaning their content cannot be changed after creation. Tuples are defined using parentheses (`()`).

***Example:***

```
point = (10, 20)  # A tuple representing a point in 2D space
person = ('Alice', 30)  # A tuple with a name and age
```

## 6. Dictionary

Dictionaries are unordered collections of key-value pairs, where each key must be unique. They are mutable and are defined using curly braces (`{}`).

***Example:***

```
student = {'name': 'Alice', 'age': 21, 'major': 'Computer
Science'}
```

## 7. Sets

Sets are unordered collections of unique items, defined using curly braces (`{}`). They are mutable, meaning items can be added or removed. Sets are useful for operations that require uniqueness, like membership tests and mathematical set operations.

***Example:***

```
unique_numbers = {1, 2, 3, 4, 4}   # Duplicates are
automatically removed
```

## 8. Literals

Literals are fixed values used in the code, representing data directly. There are several types of literals in Python:

- **Numeric Literals**: Represent numbers (e.g., 10, 3.14, 1 + 2j).
- **String Literals**: Represent strings (e.g., "hello", 'world').
- **Boolean Literals**: Represent boolean values (True, False).
- **Special Literal**: Represents the absence of a value (None).

***Example:***

```
numeric_literal = 42# An integer literal
string_literal = "Python"# A string literal
boolean_literal = True# A boolean literal
none_literal = None# A None literal
```

## Python Operators

Python operators are special symbols that perform operations on variables and values. They can be categorized into several types, each serving a specific purpose. Below is a detailed overview of the various types of operators in Python, including arithmetic, comparison, logical, bitwise, assignment, membership, and more.

### 1. Arithmetic Operators

Arithmetic operators in Python are fundamental symbols used to perform basic mathematical operations on numeric values. These operators include addition (+), subtraction (-), multiplication (*), division (/), floor division (//), modulus (%), and exponentiation (**). They allow programmers to execute a variety of calculations, such as combining numbers, finding differences, calculating products, and determining remainders or powers. For example, using 5 + 3 yields 8, while 10 % 3 results in 1, showcasing how arithmetic operators facilitate efficient mathematical processing within Python code (Table 1.4).

**Table 1.4: Arithmetic Operators and their Description with Example**

| Operator | Description | Example |
|---|---|---|
| + | Addition | a + b |
| - | Subtraction | a - b |
| * | Multiplication | a * b |
| / | Division (returns float) | a / b |
| // | Floor Division (returns integer) | a // b |
| % | Modulus (returns remainder) | a % b |
| ** | Exponentiation (power) | a ** b |

## 2. Comparison Operators

Comparison operators in Python are essential tools used to compare two values or expressions, evaluating their relational status. These operators include equal to (==), not equal to (!=), greater than (>), less than (<), greater than or equal to (>=), and less than or equal to (<=). When utilized in expressions, they return a boolean result—either True or False—indicating whether the comparison holds true. For instance, the expression 5 > 3 evaluates to True, while 4 == 5 evaluates to False. This capability is crucial in decision-making processes within programs, allowing conditional statements and control flows to execute based on the outcome of these comparisons (Table 1.5).

**Table 1.5: Comparison Operators and their Description with Example.**

| Operator | Description | Example |
|---|---|---|
| == | Equal to | a == b |
| != | Not equal to | a != b |
| > | Greater than | a > b |
| < | Less than | a < b |
| >= | Greater than or equal to | a >= b |
| <= | Less than or equal to | a <= b |

## 3. Logical Operators

Logical operators in Python are used to combine multiple conditional statements, allowing for more complex decision-making in programming. The primary logical operators are and, or, and not. The and operator returns True only if both conditions it combines are true, while the or operator returns True if at least one of the conditions is true. The not operator reverses the boolean value of a condition, returning True if the condition is false and vice versa. For example, in the expression True and False, the result is False, whereas True or False evaluates to True. Logical operators are essential for controlling the flow of a program, enabling the implementation of conditional logic based on multiple criteria (Table 1.6).

**Table 1.6: Logical Operators and their Description with Example.**

| Operator | Description | Example |
|---|---|---|
| and | Returns True if both statements are true | a and b |
| or | Returns True if at least one statement is true | a or b |
| not | Reverses the result of the statement | not a |

## 4. Bitwise Operators

Bitwise operators in Python operate at the binary level, manipulating individual bits of integer values. These operators are essential for low-level programming tasks, such as performance optimization, cryptography, and systems programming. The primary bitwise operators include AND (&), OR (|), XOR (^),

NOT (~), left shift (<<), and right shift (>>). For instance, the AND operator (&) returns a bit set to 1 only if both corresponding bits are 1, while the OR operator (|) returns 1 if at least one of the bits is 1. The NOT operator (~) inverts the bits, converting 1 to 0 and vice versa. Shifting operators (<< and >>) move bits left or right, effectively multiplying or dividing the number by two. Utilizing bitwise operators allows programmers to perform efficient calculations and control hardware directly, making them powerful tools in specific contexts where performance and resource management are critical (Table 1.7).

**Table 1.7: Bitwise Operators and their Description with Example**

| Operator | Description | Example |
|---|---|---|
| & | Bitwise AND | a & b |
| ` | ` | Bitwise OR |
| ^ | Bitwise XOR | a ^ b |
| ~ | Bitwise NOT | ~a |
| << | Left shift | a << 2 |
| >> | Right shift | a >> 2 |

### 5. Assignment Operators

Assignment operators in Python are used to assign values to variables and can also combine assignment with arithmetic operations in a single statement. The simplest assignment operator is the equals sign (=), which assigns the value on its right to the variable on its left. For example, x = 5 assigns the value 5 to the variable x. In addition to basic assignment, Python provides a range of compound assignment operators that perform an operation and then assign the result back to the variable, simplifying code and enhancing readability. These include operators like += (add and assign), -= (subtract and assign), *= (multiply and assign), and /= (divide and assign). For instance, x += 3 is equivalent to x = x + 3, effectively increasing the value of x by 3 in a more concise manner. This functionality allows developers to write more efficient and compact code while maintaining clarity.

**Table 1.8: Assignment Operators and their Description with Example**

| Operator | Description | Example |
|---|---|---|
| = | Assigns right operand to left operand | a = 10 |
| += | Add and assign | a += b |
| -= | Subtract and assign | a -= b |
| *= | Multiply and assign | a *= b |
| /= | Divide and assign | a /= b |
| %= | Modulus and assign | a %= b |
| **= | Exponentiation and assign | a **= b |
| //= | Floor division and assign | a //= b |

## 6. Membership Operators

Membership operators in Python are used to determine whether a specific value or variable exists within a sequence, such as strings, lists, tuples, or dictionaries. The two primary membership operators are in and not in. The in operator returns True if the value being tested is found within the specified sequence, while not in returns True if the value is absent. For example, in the expression "apple" in ["banana", "orange", "apple"], the result would be True because "apple" is indeed present in the list. Similarly, 3 not in (1, 2, 4) evaluates to True, indicating that 3 is not found in the tuple. These operators are particularly useful for conditional statements and loops, allowing developers to efficiently check for the presence or absence of elements within various data structures, thereby enhancing code functionality and control flow (Table 1.9).

**Table 1.9: Membership Operators and their Description with Example**

| Operator | Description | Example |
|---|---|---|
| in | Returns True if the value is found | x in list |
| not in | Returns True if the value is not found | x not in list |

## 7. Identity Operators

Identity operators in Python are used to compare the memory locations of two objects, determining whether they refer to the same object in memory rather than simply having the same value. The two primary identity operators are is and is not. The is operator returns True if both operands point to the same object, while the is not operator returns True if they do not point to the same object. For example, consider the expressions a is b and a is not b: if both a and b refer to the same object in memory, the first expression evaluates to True, whereas the second evaluates to False. This capability is particularly useful when working with mutable objects (like lists or dictionaries) where multiple variables can reference the same object, and it helps to understand how changes to one variable may affect another. Understanding identity operators is crucial for optimizing memory usage and ensuring accurate comparisons in Python programming (Table 1.10).

**Table 1.10: Identity Operators and their Description with Example**

| Operator | Description | Example |
|---|---|---|
| is | Returns True if both variables point to the same object | a is b |
| is not | Returns True if both variables do not point to the same object | a is not b |

## 8. Input and Output Statements

### *a. Input Statement*

The input () function is used to take input from the user. It always returns the input as a string.

***Example:***

```
name = input("Enter your name: ")  # Takes input from the
user
```

**b. *Output Statement***

The print() function is used to display output to the console.

***Example:***

```
print("Hello, World!")  # Prints a string to the console
```

## 9. Expressions

An expression is a combination of values, variables, operators, and calls to functions that the Python interpreter evaluates to produce a result. Expressions can be simple, like `2 + 2`, or complex, involving multiple operations and functions.

***Example:***

```
result = (3 + 5) * 2# An expression that evaluates to 16
```

Python operators enable developers to perform various operations on data. From arithmetic and comparison to logical and bitwise operations, Python provides a rich set of tools for manipulating data. Understanding these operators is crucial for effective programming, allowing for the construction of complex expressions, conditions, and control flows within applications. Input and output statements facilitate interaction with users, enhancing the usability of Python programs.

## Summary

Python, created by Guido van Rossum and released in 1991, is a high-level, versatile programming language known for its simple, readable syntax and wide applicability in various domains, including web development, data science, automation, and artificial intelligence. Its importance stems from its ease of use, extensive libraries, and vibrant community. Python's installation is straightforward, and it is available for various operating systems through the official website. Python's key components include variables, which store data; constants, which hold immutable values; identifiers, which are names assigned to variables and functions; comments, used for documenting code; and reserved keywords, which are predefined words that cannot be used as identifiers. The language offers various basic data types such as numeric types (integers and floats), strings, booleans, lists, tuples, dictionaries, sets, and literals, along with type conversion functions to switch between these types. Python also supports a rich set of operators, including arithmetic, comparison, logical, bitwise, assignment, and membership operators, used to perform operations and comparisons. Input and output are handled through input() and print() functions. These features make Python a powerful tool for both beginners and experts in programming.

## Exercise Questions

- Define a variable in Python and assign it a value of your choice. Print the value of the variable.
- What is the difference between variables and constants in Python? Demonstrate this by defining both and printing them.
- Create a Python program that takes the user's name and age as input, then displays a personalized greeting.
- Create a dictionary with at least five key-value pairs. Access and print the value associated with a specific key.
- Write a program that checks whether a given number is positive, negative, or zero using an if-else statement.
- Create a list containing different types of data (string, integer, float). Access and print the second element.
- Demonstrate type conversion by converting a float to an integer and printing the result.
- Write a Python program that asks for two numbers, adds them, and prints the result.
- Write a Python program to demonstrate the use of comparison operators by comparing two numbers.
- Use a for loop to iterate through a list of numbers and print each number squared.
- Demonstrate the use of logical operators (and, or, not) with appropriate examples.
- Create a tuple with five elements and print the last element.
- Write a Python program that checks whether a given number exists in a list using the membership operator (in).
- Convert the string "python" to uppercase and print the result.
- Write a program using input() to take a string from the user and check if it contains the word "Python" using the membership operator.

CHAPTER - 2

# Control Statements, Loops and String

Control statements in Python allow for decision-making and the execution of code blocks based on certain conditions. The primary control statements are the if-elif-else statement and the match-case statement, which help to guide the flow of a program based on various criteria.Control statements like if-elif-else and match-case play a crucial role in programming by allowing developers to implement conditional logic. The if-elif-else structure is ideal for simpler conditions, while the match-case statement offers advanced pattern matching capabilities, making it easier to write clear and concise code for handling multiple conditions. These constructs enhance the readability and maintainability of Python programs, enabling developers to control the flow of execution effectively.

## 1. If-Elif-Else Statement

The if-elif-else statement is a fundamental control structure used for conditional execution. It evaluates a condition and executes a specific block of code if the condition is true. If the condition is false, it can check additional conditions using elif (short for "else if") and execute the corresponding block if one of those conditions is true. If none of the conditions are met, the code in the else block will execute.

***Syntax:***

```
if condition1:
  # Execute block of code if condition1 is true
elif condition2:
  # Execute block of code if condition2 is true
else:
  # Execute block of code if neither condition1 nor condition2
is true
```

***Example:***

```
age = 20
if age < 13:
  print("Child")
elif age < 18:
  print("Teenager")
else:
 print("Adult")
```

In this example, the program checks the value of age and prints out the corresponding age category.

## 2. Match-Case Statement

Introduced in Python 3.10, the match-case statement provides a more powerful and flexible way to handle conditional logic, resembling the switch-case statements found in other programming languages. It allows matching against patterns, making it easier to handle complex conditions and data structures.

***Syntax:***

```
match variable:
    case pattern1:
        # Execute block of code for pattern1
    case pattern2:
        # Execute block of code for pattern2
    case _:
        # Default case if no patterns match
```

***Example:***

```
def describe_color(color):
    match color:
        case "red":
            return "Color of passion"
        case "green":
            return "Color of nature
```

```
case "blue":
            return "Color of the sky"
        case _:
            return "Unknown color"
print(describe_color("green"))  # Output: Color of nature
```

In this example, the match statement evaluates the color variable against multiple patterns, executing the corresponding code block based on the match. If no match is found, the default case (using _) is executed.

## Loops

Loops in Python are control structures that allow code to be executed repeatedly based on a condition or over a sequence of items. The two primary types of loops in Python are the while loop and the for loop, and both can be combined with control statements like break, continue, and pass to manage the flow of execution.

### 1. While Loop

The while loop repeatedly executes a block of code as long as a specified condition is true. It is useful when the number of iterations is not known beforehand.

***Syntax:***

```
while condition:
    # Code block to be executed
```

***Example:***

```
count = 0
while count < 5:
    print(count)
    count += 1
```

In this example, the loop prints numbers from 0 to 4. The loop continues until the condition (count < 5) becomes false.

### 2. For Loop

The for loop iterates over a sequence (like a list, tuple, string, or range) and executes a block of code for each item in the sequence. It is useful for iterating over a known number of items.

***Syntax:***

```
for variable in sequence:
    # Code block to be executed
```

***Example:***

```
fruits = ["apple", "banana", "cherry"]
for fruit in fruits:
    print(fruit)
```

In this example, the loop prints each fruit in the list, iterating over the sequence.

### 3. Nested Loops

Nested loops are loops that exist within another loop. This structure allows for the iteration of multiple sequences or dimensions.

***Syntax:***

```
for outer_variable in outer_sequence:
    for inner_variable in inner_sequence:
        # Code block to be executed
```

***Example:***

```
for i in range(3):  # Outer loop
    for j in range(2):  # Inner loop
        print(f"i: {i}, j: {j}")
```

In this example, the outer loop runs three times, and for each iteration of the outer loop, the inner loop runs twice, producing pairs of i and j.

### 4. Break Statement

The break statement is used to exit a loop prematurely. When encountered, it terminates the loop, and execution continues with the statement immediately following the loop.

***Example:***

```
for num in range(10):
    if num == 5:
        break
    print(num)
```

In this example, the loop prints numbers from 0 to 4, and when num reaches 5, the loop exits.

### 5. Continue Statement

The continue statement skips the current iteration of a loop and proceeds to the next iteration. It allows for selective skipping of certain iterations based on conditions.

***Example:***

```
for num in range(5):
    if num == 2:
        continue
    print(num)
```

In this example, the number 2 is skipped, and the loop prints 0, 1, 3, and 4.

### 6. Pass Statement

The pass statement serves as a placeholder in Python. It does nothing when executed and is typically used in situations where a statement is syntactically required but no action is needed. It can be useful for implementing future code or during development.

***Example:***

```
for num in range(5):
    if num == 2:
        pass  # Placeholder for future code
    print(num)
```

In this example, the pass statement is executed when num is 2, but it doesn't affect the loop's functionality, allowing it to print all numbers from 0 to 4.

Loops in Python, including while and for loops, allow for repetitive execution of code blocks, enhancing efficiency and reducing redundancy. Control statements like break, continue, and pass provide additional flexibility, enabling developers to manage loop behavior effectively. Understanding these constructs is essential for writing efficient and organized code in Python

## String

Strings in Python are fundamental data types that represent sequences of characters, used extensively for handling textual data. They can be created using single, double, or triple quotes, enabling flexibility in how text is represented, including multi-line strings. Python strings offer a wide range of built-in methods and functionalities that facilitate effective manipulation and analysis, such as indexing and slicing for accessing specific characters or substrings, concatenation for combining multiple strings, and methods for searching, replacing, splitting, and joining strings. Additionally, developers can change the case of strings, check for specific prefixes or suffixes, and perform various other operations, making strings a versatile and essential component in Python programming for text processing and data management. Below is a detailed overview of key string operations in Python.

### 1. Creating Strings

Strings in Python can be created by enclosing characters in single quotes ('), double quotes ("), or triple quotes (''' or """) for multi-line strings.

***Examples:***

```
single_quote_string = 'Hello, World!'
double_quote_string = "Hello, World!"
triple_quote_string = '''This is a multi-line
string.'''
```

### 2. Length of a String

The length of a string, or the number of characters it contains, can be determined using the len() function.

***Example:***

```
my_string = "Hello"
length = len(my_string)  # Output: 5
```

### 3. Indexing and Slicing in Strings

Strings are indexed, meaning each character has a position starting from 0. You can access specific characters using indexing or extract a substring using slicing.

***Example:***

```
my_string = "Python"
first_character = my_string[0]  # Output: 'P'
substring = my_string[1:4]       # Output: 'yth'
```

## 4. Concatenation of Strings

Strings can be combined using the + operator, known as concatenation. This allows you to merge multiple strings into one.

***Example:***

```
string1 = "Hello"
string2 = "World"
combined_string = string1 + " " + string2  # Output: 'Hello
World'
```

## 5. Finding Substring

To determine if a substring exists within a string, the in operator can be used. You can also utilize the find() method to locate the position of a substring.

***Example:***

```
my_string = "Hello, World!"
contains_world = "World" in my_string  # Output: True
position = my_string.find("World")      # Output: 7
```

## 6. Splitting and Joining Strings

The split() method breaks a string into a list of substrings based on a specified delimiter. Conversely, the join() method combines a list of strings into a single string using a specified separator.

***Example:***

```
my_string = "apple,banana,cherry"
split_string = my_string.split(",")     # Output: ['apple',
'banana', 'cherry']
joined_string = ", ".join(split_string)  # Output: 'apple,
banana, cherry'
```

## 7. Changing Case of a String

Strings can be modified to different cases using methods such as lower(), upper(), title(), and capitalize().

***Example:***

```
my_string = "Hello World"
lower_case = my_string.lower()      # Output: 'hello world'
upper_case = my_string.upper()      # Output: 'HELLO WORLD'
title_case = my_string.title()      # Output: 'Hello World'
```

## 8. Checking Starting and Ending of a String

To check if a string starts or ends with a specific substring, you can use the startswith() and endswith() methods.

***Example:***

```
my_string = "Python programming"
starts_with_python   =   my_string.startswith("Python")   #
Output: True
ends_with_programming   =   my_string.endswith("Java")   #
Output: False
```

## 9. Inserting Substring into a String

While strings in Python are immutable (cannot be changed in place), you can create a new string by inserting a substring using concatenation.

***Example:***

```
my_string = "Python programming"
inserted_string = my_string[:7] + "is fun, " + my_string[7:]
# Output: 'Python is fun, program
```

## Summary

Control statements in Python, such as if-elif-else and match-case, allow developers to implement decision-making in code. The if-elif-else statement evaluates conditions and executes corresponding blocks of code based on boolean expressions. The match-case statement (introduced in Python 3.10) provides a more powerful and readable way to perform pattern matching, especially with complex data structures. Python also includes looping mechanisms such as while and for loops, which are used for repeating tasks. Loops can be controlled with break (to exit the loop), continue (to skip the current iteration), and pass (which does nothing, often used as a placeholder). String manipulation in Python is extensive, supporting operations like string creation, length calculation, indexing, and slicing. Strings can be concatenated, checked for substrings, split, and joined. Furthermore, strings can have their case changed, and methods like startswith() and endswith() allow checking the beginning and end of strings. Additionally, inserting substrings into strings is easy with string concatenation.

## Exercise Questions

- Write a Python program using an if-elif-else statement to check if a number is positive, negative, or zero.
- Write a program using a match-case statement to match different fruit names and print a message corresponding to the fruit.
- Create a while loop that prints all numbers from 1 to 10.
- Write a for loop that iterates through a list of numbers and prints each one squared.
- Write a program that uses a nested loop to print a multiplication table from 1 to 5.
- Create a program that uses break to exit a loop once a specific condition is met (e.g., exit when the number 5 is encountered).
- Write a Python program that uses continue to skip even numbers in a range of 1 to 10.
- Implement a program that uses pass in a function or class definition where the body of the function is empty.
- Write a Python program that counts the length of a string without using the built-in len() function.
- Given a string, demonstrate how to extract a substring from index 2 to 5 using slicing.
- Concatenate two strings in Python and print the result.
- Write a program that checks if a substring exists within a string using the in operator.
- Split a string into a list of words and print each word.
- Write a Python program that converts a string to uppercase and lowercase using upper() and lower().

Check if a string starts with a specific prefix and ends with a specific suffix using startswith() and endswith().

CHAPTER - 3

# Lists & Tupples

Python offers a variety of built-in data structures that are fundamental for organizing and manipulating data efficiently. The primary data structures include lists, tuples, sets, and dictionaries. Lists are ordered, mutable collections that allow duplicate elements and are versatile for various operations, such as adding, removing, and accessing items. Tuples are similar to lists but are immutable, making them ideal for fixed collections of items that should not be altered. Sets are unordered collections of unique elements, useful for eliminating duplicates and performing mathematical operations like unions and intersections. Dictionaries, or associative arrays, are key-value pairs that enable fast retrieval of data based on a unique key, making them highly efficient for lookup operations.These data structures provide different advantages depending on the context of use. Lists are often employed for maintaining ordered sequences, while tuples can be used for fixed data collections, such as representing coordinates or records. Sets are optimal for membership testing and eliminating duplicates in datasets. Dictionaries shine when there is a need for quick access to data based on a specific identifier, allowing for efficient storage and retrieval. Understanding these data structures and their characteristics is essential for Python programming, as they form the backbone of effective data manipulation and algorithm implementation (Figure 3.1).

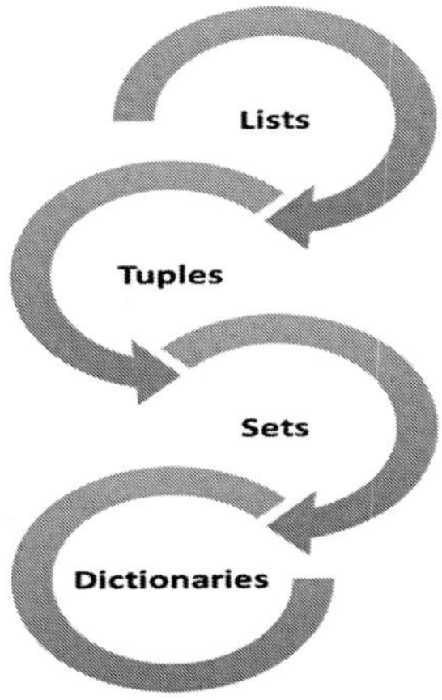


**Figure 3.1: Python Data Structures**

# Lists

## Characteristics of Lists

Lists in Python are one of the most versatile data structures, as they can store a mix of different data types like integers, strings, floating-point numbers, or even other lists. This flexibility makes them ideal for grouping and managing related data in a single, ordered sequence. Lists maintain the order in which elements are added, which allows for indexing and accessing elements by position. This property is especially useful when the sequence of items matters, such as in a to-do list or a series of measurements taken over time. Another significant characteristic is that lists allow duplicates, so the same value can appear multiple times without any restrictions, enabling use cases where repeated values are necessary.

Lists are also mutable, meaning that their contents can be changed after creation. This mutability makes lists dynamic, so their size can grow or shrink as elements are added, removed, or modified. For instance, lists support operations like appending new elements, inserting elements at specific positions, and removing elements either by value or position. This dynamic nature is beneficial for tasks that require flexible data storage and frequent modification, such as storing user inputs or continuously updating real-time data. The mutability of lists, combined with their ordered and flexible structure, makes them a powerful tool in Python for a wide range of applications.

## Creating a List

Creating a list in Python is simple and can be done by placing elements inside square brackets [], separated by commas. For example, my_list = [1, 2, 3, "apple", True] creates a list containing integers, a string, and a boolean value. Lists can store elements of any data type, making them flexible for a range of applications. An empty list can be created using my_list = [] or my_list = list(), allowing you to add elements later as needed. Lists can also be generated dynamically, such as by using loops or list comprehensions, which makes it easy to populate lists with values programmatically.

***For example:***

```
my_list = [1, 2, 3, "apple", True]
An empty list can be created with my_list = [] or my_list
= list().
```

## Indexing and Slicing

Lists support indexing, where each item has a position (starting from 0 for the first element). For example, my_list[0] gives the first element. Negative indexing allows access from the end (-1 gives the last element). Slicing is used to access a range of items, such as my_list[1:3] for elements from index 1 to 2 (excluding 3).

### *Operations on Lists*

Lists support various operations like concatenation (+), repetition (*), and membership testing (in).

***For example:***

```
combined_list = [1, 2] + [3, 4]  # [1, 2, 3, 4]
repeated_list = [0] * 3          # [0, 0, 0]
```

### *List Methods*

Python provides numerous methods to manipulate lists:

- append(): Adds an element at the end.
- insert(index, item): Inserts an item at a specified position.
- remove(item): Removes the first occurrence of an item.
- pop(): Removes and returns the last item (or item at a given index).
- sort(): Sorts the list in ascending or descending order.
- reverse(): Reverses the list order.

### *List Comprehension*

List comprehension offers a concise way to create lists by applying an expression to each element in an iterable.

***For example:***

```
squared_numbers = [x ** 2 for x in range(5)]  # [0, 1, 4,
9, 16]
```

This approach is often faster and more readable for simple transformations or filtering of lists.

## Tuples

Tuples in Python are ordered, immutable collections that can store elements of any data type, including integers, strings, and even other tuples. Defined using parentheses ()—for example, my_tuple = (1, "apple", 3.14)—they preserve the order of elements, similar to lists, but cannot be modified once created. This immutability makes tuples ideal for storing data that should remain constant, such as coordinates, days of the week, or configuration settings. Tuples also allow for faster access than lists and are often used to improve performance in scenarios where data integrity is important. They support indexing, slicing, and basic operations like concatenation and repetition.

## Tuples vs lists

Tuples and lists are two essential data structures in Python, each with unique features suited to different use cases.

Lists are mutable, meaning you can modify, add, or remove elements after the list is created. They're created using square brackets [], like my_list = [1, 2, 3]. This flexibility makes lists ideal for dynamic collections that may change over time, such as a list of user inputs or items in a shopping cart. Lists also come with a wide range of built-in methods (e.g., append(), remove(), sort()) that make it easy to manage and organize data.

Tuples, on the other hand, are immutable; once a tuple is created, its elements cannot be changed, added, or removed. Defined using parentheses (), such as my_tuple = (1, 2, 3), tuples are often used for data that should remain constant, like coordinates or configuration settings. Tuples are generally faster to access than lists and use slightly less memory due to their fixed structure, making them a better choice for performance-sensitive situations.

## Tuples vs. Lists in Python

**Tuples** and **lists** are both fundamental data structures in Python, but they serve different purposes due to their unique characteristics. Here's a detailed comparison (Table 3.1).

### 1. Mutability:

- **Lists** are mutable, meaning you can modify them after creation (add, remove, or change elements).
- **Tuples** are immutable, so once they are created, their elements cannot be changed, added, or removed. This immutability makes tuples a safer choice for storing fixed data.

### 2. Syntax:

- **Lists** are defined with square brackets [], like my_list = [1, 2, 3].
- **Tuples** are defined with parentheses (), like my_tuple = (1, 2, 3).

### 3. Use Case:

- **Lists** are generally used for collections of data that are expected to change or grow over time. For example, lists are ideal for maintaining dynamic datasets, such as a list of items in a shopping cart.
- **Tuples** are best used when the data should remain constant. Common examples include geographical coordinates, dates, or fixed configuration values.

### 4. Performance:

- **Tuples** are generally faster than lists, especially when accessing elements, due to their immutability.
- **Lists** are slower in comparison but allow for flexibility due to mutability.

### 5. Memory Efficiency:

- **Tuples** consume slightly less memory than lists because they don't require extra memory allocation for modifying contents.
- **Lists** require additional memory management due to their dynamic nature.

### 6. Methods Available:

- Lists come with many methods, such as append(), remove(), pop(), and sort(), which support modification and organization of data.
- Tuples have only a few built-in methods, like count() and index(), since they cannot be modified after creation.

### 7. Unpacking:

- Both **lists** and **tuples** support unpacking, allowing for the assignment of elements to variables directly, like a, b, c = (1, 2, 3).

**Table 3.1: Comparison of Lists and Tuples**

| Feature | Lists | Tuples |
|---|---|---|
| **Mutability** | Mutable (modifiable) | Immutable (non-modifiable) |
| **Syntax** | Square brackets [] | Parentheses () |
| **Use Case** | Dynamic collections | Fixed, constant collections |
| **Performance** | Slower than tuples | Faster than lists |
| **Memory Efficiency** | Uses more memory | Uses less memory |
| **Methods Available** | Extensive (append, pop) | Limited (count, index) |
| **Unpacking Support** | Yes | Yes |

**Use lists** when you need a flexible, changeable collection, and **use tuples** when you need a fixed, unchangeable collection for faster access and efficient memory use.

## Creating and Accessing Tuples

### *Creating Tuples*

Tuples in Python can be created by placing elements within parentheses (), separated by commas.

***For example:***

```
my_tuple = (1, 2, 3, "apple", True)
```

This creates a tuple with five elements of different data types. Unlike lists, once created, tuples cannot be modified (they are immutable). You can also create a tuple without parentheses by simply separating items with commas:

```
my_tuple = 1, 2, 3  # This is also a tuple
```

For a tuple with a single item, you need a trailing comma to distinguish it from a regular value:

```
single_item_tuple = (42,)
```

### *Accessing Tuple Elements*

Tuple elements are accessed using indexing, similar to lists. The index of the first item is 0, the second is 1, and so on. For example:

```
my_tuple = (10, 20, 30, 40)
print(my_tuple[0])  # Output: 10
```

You can also use negative indexing to access elements from the end of the tuple, where -1 refers to the last element:

```
print(my_tuple[-1])  # Output: 40
```

### *Slicing Tuples*

Tuples support slicing to access a range of elements. This is done using the start:stop syntax:

```
my_tuple = (1, 2, 3, 4, 5)
print(my_tuple[1:4])  # Output: (2, 3, 4)
```

Slicing works similarly to lists, where start is inclusive, and stop is exclusive. You can also omit start or stop to get elements from the beginning or up to the end of the tuple, respectively

This Table3.2. gives a quick guide on how to create and access tuple elements in Python.

**Table 3.2: Summary Table**

| Operation | Example Code | Description |
|---|---|---|
| Basic Creation | my_tuple = (1, 2, 3) | Creates a tuple with multiple elements |
| Without Parentheses | my_tuple = 1, 2, 3 | Creates a tuple without parentheses |
| Single Item Tuple | single_item_tuple = (42,) | Trailing comma needed for single-element tuple |
| Indexing | my_tuple[0] | Accesses the first element |
| Negative Indexing | my_tuple[-1] | Accesses the last element |
| Slicing | my_tuple[1:3] | Accesses elements from index 1 to 2 |
| Access Entire Tuple | print(my_tuple[:]) | Returns a copy of the entire tuple |

## Tuple Operations and Methods

Tuples in Python are immutable, which means their elements cannot be changed, added, or removed after the tuple is created. However, despite this immutability, tuples still support several useful operations that allow us to work with their data effectively. For example, tuples can be concatenated using the + operator, which joins two or more tuples into a new one without altering the original tuples. Similarly, tuples can be repeated with the * operator, creating a new tuple with repeated elements, useful for cases where you want multiple copies of the same data. You can also check if an element exists within a tuple using the in keyword, which performs a membership test, returning True if the element is found.

Although tuples have limited built-in methods compared to lists, they still offer two essential methods: count() and index(). The count() method returns the number of occurrences of a specific value, which can be helpful for analyzing data. The index() method finds the first position of a specified value, which is useful for locating elements. Additionally, since tuples support iteration, you can loop through each element in a tuple using a for loop, allowing easy access to each item for operations such as printing or performing calculations. These capabilities make tuples highly efficient for managing fixed collections of data, providing a balance of immutability with useful methods for data handling.

### *Common Tuple Operations*

**Concatenation:** Tuples can be joined using the + operator.

```
tuple1 = (1, 2, 3)
tuple2 = (4, 5, 6)
result = tuple1 + tuple2  # Output: (1, 2, 3, 4, 5, 6)
```

**Repetition:** You can repeat a tuple multiple times using the * operator.

```
tuple1 = (1, 2, 3)
result = tuple1 * 3  # Output: (1, 2, 3, 1, 2, 3, 1, 2, 3)
```

**Membership Testing:** The in keyword can be used to check if an element exists in a tuple.

```
tuple1 = (1, 2, 3)
print(2 in tuple1)  # Output: True
```

### *Tuple Methods*

Since tuples are immutable, they only support a few methods:

**count():** Returns the number of times a specified value appears in the tuple.

```
tuple1 = (1, 2, 2, 3)
print(tuple1.count(2))  # Output: 2
```

**index():** Returns the index of the first occurrence of a specified value.

```
tuple1 = (1, 2, 3, 2)
print(tuple1.index(2))  # Output: 1
```

### *Iterating Over Tuples*

Tuples can be easily iterated over with a for loop, just like lists. This is useful for accessing each element one by one or performing operations with each element.

```
my_tuple = (1, 2, 3, 4)
for item in my_tuple:
    print(item)  # Output: 1, 2, 3, 4 on separate lines
```

## Summary

In Python, lists are ordered, mutable collections that can store multiple elements, including other lists. They are characterized by their ability to hold heterogeneous data types and can be manipulated using indexing, slicing, and various operations. Common list methods include append(), remove(), insert(), and pop(), among others, which enable users to modify the list efficiently. List comprehension is a powerful feature that allows the creation of lists using concise syntax, often making code more readable and efficient. On the other hand, tuples are similar to lists in that they can store multiple elements, but they are immutable, meaning once they are created, they cannot be changed. Tuples are typically used for storing fixed data that should not be altered. While tuples offer methods like count() and index(), they are not as flexible as lists for data manipulation. Lists support more operations, such as item deletion or modification, while tuples focus on data integrity. Both can be iterated over using loops, though tuples are more memory efficient due to their immutability.

## Exercise Questions

- Create a list containing five integers. Print the first and last elements using indexing.
- Slice a list of numbers to get a sublist containing the second through the fourth elements.
- Use the append() method to add a new element to a list and print the updated list.
- Remove an element from a list using the remove() method and print the result.
- Write a program that demonstrates the use of list comprehension to create a list of squares of numbers from 1 to 10.
- Create a tuple containing three strings and print the second element.
- Compare a tuple and a list. Write a program to show the key difference by attempting to modify each of them.
- Use the count() method to count how many times a specific value appears in a tuple.
- Write a Python program that finds the index of a given element in a tuple using the index() method.
- Write a program that checks whether an element exists in a tuple using the in operator.
- Create a nested list and print a specific element from a sublist using indexing.
- Iterate over a tuple using a for loop and print each element.
- Create a list and use slicing to reverse the list.
- Write a Python program to convert a list into a tuple and print it.

Demonstrate how to use the insert() method to add an element to a specific index in a list.

CHAPTER - 4

# Sets and Dictionires

## Sets:

In Python, sets are a built-in data type that stores unique, unordered elements, meaning they don't preserve order and don't allow duplicate values. This uniqueness constraint makes sets highly useful for operations that require only distinct items, such as removing duplicates from a list. Sets are mutable, so you can add or remove items after creation. Common set methods include add() to add elements, remove() to delete them, and discard(), which removes an item if it exists without throwing an error if it doesn't. Membership tests (e.g., item in set) are also efficient in sets, as they are implemented using hash tables, allowing for fast lookups.

Sets are also ideal for various mathematical operations like union, intersection, difference, and symmetric difference. For example, the union() method combines all unique elements from multiple sets, while intersection() finds elements common to all sets involved. These operations are handy for tasks like filtering unique data or finding shared elements across datasets. Python also provides frozenset, an immutable version of sets, which is useful when a hashable collection type is needed for use as dictionary keys or elements in other sets. The versatility of sets and their efficiency in handling unique data make them a valuable tool in data processing and organization.

Here's a complete appearance at how to create, modify, operate on, and iterate over sets in Python.

### Creating and Modifying Sets

*Creating Sets:* Creating sets in Python is simple and can be done using curly braces {} or the set() function. When you use curly braces, Python automatically removes any duplicate elements, so the set only contains unique values. For example, {1, 2, 3, 3} will result in {1, 2, 3} because duplicates are discarded. You can also create an empty set using set() (note that {} would create an empty dictionary, not a set). Sets can contain mixed data types, as long as they are hashable (immutable types like integers, strings, and tuples are allowed, while lists or other sets are not).

```
my_set = {1, 2, 3, 4, 4}  # Output: {1, 2, 3, 4}
empty_set = set()  # Creates an empty set; {} creates an empty dictionary
```

***Adding Elements:*** Since sets in Python are mutable, you can add elements to them after they are created using the add() method. This method allows you to insert a single, unique element into the set. If the element already exists in the set, add() will simply ignore it, maintaining the set's property of unique values.

***For example:***

```
my_set = {1, 2, 3}
my_set.add(4)  # Now my_set becomes {1, 2, 3, 4}
my_set.add(3)  # No change, as 3 is already in the set
```

Using add() is efficient for adding single elements but does not support adding multiple elements at once. For adding multiple items, the update() method is more appropriate.

***Updating Sets:*** The update() method in Python is used to add multiple elements to a set efficiently. It accepts an iterable as an argument, which can be a list, tuple, or even another set, and it incorporates all unique elements from the iterable into the existing set. This method modifies the original set in place and ensures that any duplicate elements from the iterable are ignored, maintaining the set's property of containing only unique items. For example, calling my_set.update([1, 2, 3]) on a set that already contains {2, 3} would result in the set being updated to {1, 2, 3}, as it adds 1 and ignores 2 and 3 since they are already present.

```
my_set = {1, 2, 3}
my_set.update([4, 5, 6])  # Output: {1, 2, 3, 4, 5, 6}
```

***Removing Elements:***

- remove(element): Removes the specified element from the set. Raises an error if the element is not found.
- discard(element): Also removes the specified element, but does not raise an error if the element isn't in the set.
- pop(): Removes and returns an arbitrary element from the set (since sets are unordered).
- clear(): Empties the set.

```
my_set = {1, 2, 3}
my_set.remove(2)  # Output: {1, 3}
my_set.discard(5) # No error, even though 5 isn't in the set
my_set.pop()      # Removes a random element
my_set.clear()    # Results in an empty set
```

### *Set Operations*

Sets support a range of operations that are particularly useful for tasks involving unique collections and comparisons. Common operations include union, intersection, difference, and symmetric difference.

Union (|): Combines all elements from two sets (removing duplicates).

```
set1 = {1, 2, 3}
set2 = {3, 4, 5}
union_set = set1 | set2  # Output: {1, 2, 3, 4, 5}
```

Intersection (&): Finds common elements between two sets.

```
intersection_set = set1 & set2  # Output: {3}
```

Difference (-): Returns elements in the first set that aren't in the second set.

```
difference_set = set1 - set2  # Output: {1, 2}
```

Symmetric Difference (^): Returns elements in either set but not in both.

```
symmetric_diff_set = set1 ^ set2  # Output: {1, 2, 4, 5}
```

### *Set Methods*

Python sets have several built-in methods for advanced set operations and comparisons.

```
isdisjoint(): Checks if two sets have no elements in common.
set1.isdisjoint(set2)  # Output: False
```

issubset(): Checks if one set is a subset of another.

```
set1.issubset(set2)  # Output: False
```

issuperset(): Checks if one set is a superset of another.

```
set1.issuperset({1, 2})  # Output: True
copy(): Creates a shallow copy of the set.
new_set = set1.copy()
```

### Iterating Over Sets

You can use a for loop to iterate over the elements of a set. Since sets are unordered, elements will appear in an arbitrary order each time you iterate.

```
my_set = {1, 2, 3, 4}
for item in my_set:
    print(item)  # Output: Elements in arbitrary order
```

Sets are a powerful data structure for handling collections of unique elements, enabling efficient membership testing, mathematical set operations, and more (Table 4.1).

**Table 4.1: Sets operation with Example**

| Operation/ Method | Example Code | Description |
|---|---|---|
| **Create Set** | my_set = {1, 2, 3} | Creates a set with unique elements |
| **Add Element** | my_set.add(4) | Adds an element to the set |
| **Update Set** | my_set.update([4, 5, 6]) | Adds multiple elements from an iterable |
| **Remove Element** | my_set.remove(2) | Removes specified element (raises error if not found) |
| **Union** | `set1 | set2` |
| **Intersection** | set1 & set2 | Finds common elements in both sets |
| **Difference** | set1 - set2 | Finds elements in first set, not in second |
| **Symmetric Difference** | set1 ^ set2 | Finds elements in either set, but not both |
| **isdisjoint()** | set1.isdisjoint(set2) | Checks if two sets have no elements in common |
| **issubset()** | set1.issubset(set2) | Checks if all elements of set1 are in set2 |
| **issuperset()** | set1. issuperset(set2) | Checks if all elements of set2 are in set1 |
| **Iteration** | for item in my_set | Loops through each element of the set |

## Dictionaries

Dictionaries in Python are a built-in data type that serves as a collection of key-value pairs, where each key is unique and is used to access its associated value.

This data structure is defined using curly braces {} or the dict() constructor, allowing for an efficient way to store and retrieve data. Each key must be immutable (such as strings, numbers, or tuples), while the values can be of any data type, including other dictionaries. This flexibility makes dictionaries a powerful tool for representing structured data, such as JSON objects or records from a database. One of the main advantages of using dictionaries is their fast average time complexity for lookups, inserts, and deletes, which is approximately O(1). This performance is achieved through hashing, where keys are transformed into hash values to quickly locate corresponding values. Dictionaries also provide various methods for manipulating data, such as get() for safe retrieval of values, keys() to obtain a list of keys, and items() to iterate through key-value pairs. Overall, dictionaries are an essential part of Python programming, widely used for tasks ranging from simple data storage to complex data manipulation and analysis.

## Characteristics of Dictionaries

Dictionaries in Python are versatile and powerful data structures characterized by several distinct features that set them apart from other collection types like lists and sets (Figure 4.1).

*Here are the key characteristics of dictionaries explained in detail:*

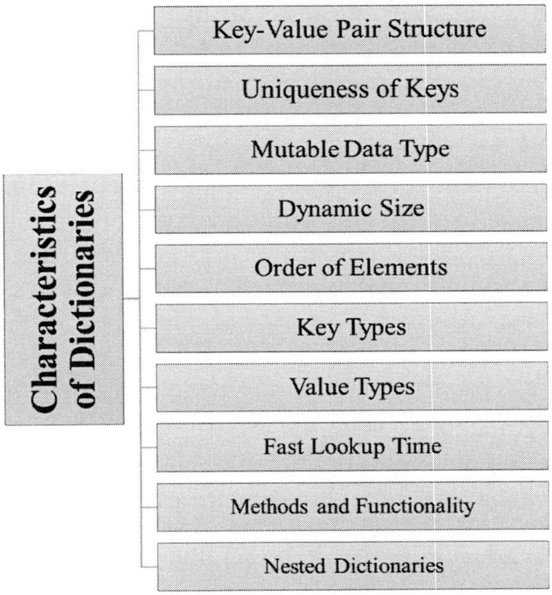


**Figure 4.1: Characteristics of Dictionaries**

### Key-Value Pair Structure:

A dictionary in Python is a collection of key-value pairs, where each unique key is associated with a specific value. This structure enables quick data retrieval because, unlike lists or tuples, you can directly access the value associated with a given key rather than searching through all items sequentially. Keys in a dictionary must be immutable types (like strings, numbers, or tuples), while values can be any data type. This flexibility makes dictionaries ideal for various applications, such as storing and organizing data by unique identifiers, counting occurrences, and handling data that requires fast lookups. Dictionary operations like adding, updating, and deleting key-value pairs are efficient, making dictionaries a powerful tool for structured data management.

### Uniqueness of Keys:

In Python dictionaries, each key must be unique, and if you attempt to assign a new value to an existing key, it will overwrite the previous value. This behavior ensures that each key is mapped to a single, definitive value. This feature is particularly useful when you want to update information without duplicating entries, as the dictionary will automatically manage any duplicate keys by retaining only the latest value associated with each one. This unique-key structure is fundamental to dictionaries, as it maintains the integrity of the data, allowing for quick lookups and ensuring that each key has only one corresponding value at any time.

### Mutable Data Type:

Dictionaries in Python are mutable, meaning they can be modified after creation to adapt to changing data requirements. You can easily add new key-value pairs by assigning a value to a new key, update existing pairs by reassigning values to current keys, or remove pairs using methods like del or pop(). This mutability makes dictionaries ideal for scenarios where data needs to be dynamically managed or updated frequently. For instance, dictionaries can be used to count occurrences of items, manage configurations, or track changing states within an application. The flexibility to modify entries makes dictionaries powerful for real-time data management, enabling efficient and adaptable solutions in Python programs.

### Dynamic Size:

Dictionaries in Python are dynamic, allowing their size to change as key-value pairs are added or removed. Unlike fixed-size structures, such as arrays, dictionaries can expand to accommodate new entries or shrink when entries are removed, with only memory availability as a constraint. This adaptability makes dictionaries highly versatile, as they can manage both small datasets and large, complex mappings without needing to pre-allocate a specific size. By handling resizing internally, Python's dictionary structure provides efficient storage and access, enabling developers to focus on data manipulation without worrying about capacity limits. This dynamic resizing is particularly advantageous in data-intensive applications, where the amount of data may vary over time.

### Order of Elements:

Starting with Python 3.7, dictionaries preserve the insertion order of elements, meaning that items remain in the order they were added. This feature makes dictionaries more predictable when iterating over them, as they now maintain a stable sequence that reflects their entry order. Originally a feature of the OrderedDict class, this behavior is now standard for all dictionaries, simplifying use cases where ordered data is essential. When elements are added or removed, the dictionary updates to retain the sequence of entries accordingly, enhancing both functionality and readability in data operations that rely on consistent ordering. This change aligns dictionaries more closely with ordered data structures while retaining the efficiency of traditional hash-based operations.

### Key Types:

In Python dictionaries, keys must be immutable types—such as strings, numbers, or tuples—to allow consistent hashing, a key requirement for efficient key lookup and storage. Immutability ensures that the value of each key remains constant over time, allowing the dictionary to maintain a stable reference to each key's memory address. This stability is crucial because dictionaries rely on hash values, which are generated from keys when entries are created. If a key were mutable, any change to its value would alter its hash, disrupting the dictionary's ability to locate or retrieve the corresponding entry accurately. By restricting keys to immutable types, Python ensures both data integrity and efficiency, as dictionary operations can consistently and predictably map each key to its respective value.

### Value Types:

In Python dictionaries, values associated with keys can be of any data type, allowing for the inclusion of complex and flexible data structures. Unlike keys, which must be immutable to ensure stable referencing, values can be mutable types, such as lists, other dictionaries, or sets. This flexibility enables the nesting of various data types within a dictionary, allowing for intricate structures where each key points to a unique, potentially complex value. For instance, you can create a dictionary where each key represents a student's name and each value is a list of their grades, or a dictionary of dictionaries that organizes data hierarchically. This capability supports diverse applications, from organizing configurations and user profiles to managing structured data like JSON. By accommodating mutable types, dictionaries serve as highly adaptable data structures suited for organizing and retrieving detailed data configurations efficiently.

### Fast Lookup Time:

Dictionaries provide average-case constant time complexity, O(1), for lookups, inserts, and deletions. This efficiency is achieved through hashing, which converts keys into hash values to quickly locate the associated values.

### Methods and Functionality:

Python dictionaries come with a variety of built-in methods that enhance their usability. For instance, methods like get(), keys(), values(), and items() facilitate safe access and retrieval of data, allowing for easy iteration over keys and values.

### Nested Dictionaries:

Dictionaries in Python can be nested, meaning you can use one dictionary as the value for a key in another dictionary. This powerful feature enables the creation of complex, hierarchical data structures. For example, you can create a dictionary where each key represents a category, and each value is another dictionary that holds more specific information about that category. This nesting allows for the organization of data in a tree-like structure, making it possible to represent complex models like JSON objects or multi-level configurations. Nested dictionaries are often used in applications involving structured data, such as storing user profiles with multiple attributes, managing configurations with sub-settings, or organizing items within categories in a database. This flexibility is crucial for working with data that has multiple levels of detail, making dictionaries a versatile tool for hierarchical data representation.

## Key-value Pairs

Key-value pairs are a fundamental concept in various data structures, particularly in dictionaries (or associative arrays) in programming languages like Python. This structure allows for the efficient organization and retrieval of data. Key-value pairs are a powerful and flexible way to organize and manage data. Their unique structure supports fast access, intuitive data organization, and dynamic updates, making them essential for various applications in programming and data management. Understanding how to effectively use key-value pairs is crucial for leveraging dictionaries and similar data structures in software development.

### *Definition*

A key-value pair consists of two linked elements: the key and the value. The key acts as a unique identifier for the value it is associated with, enabling quick access to the value based on the key. This pairing creates a mapping relationship, allowing data to be stored and retrieved in a structured manner.

### *Characteristics of Key-Value Pairs*

Uniqueness of Keys:In a dictionary, each key must be unique. This means that no two keys can be the same. If a new key-value pair is added with a key that already exists, the existing value is overwritten with the new value. This property ensures that each key points to exactly one value, maintaining clarity in data representation.

**Associative Nature:** Key-value pairs establish an associative relationship, where each key is directly linked to a corresponding value. This allows for intuitive data retrieval; given a key, the associated value can be quickly accessed without needing to search through other elements.

**Key Types:** Keys must be of an immutable data type, such as strings, numbers, or tuples. This immutability is critical because it ensures the stability and reliability of the key, allowing the dictionary to maintain accurate mappings without risk of modification.

**Value Types:** The values in key-value pairs can be of any data type, including mutable types like lists, dictionaries, or objects. This versatility allows for the representation of complex data structures within a single dictionary.

### *Advantages of Using Key-Value Pairs*

**Fast Access and Lookup:** The primary advantage of key-value pairs is their ability to facilitate fast data retrieval. Using a key, you can access the associated value in constant time, O(1), thanks to the underlying hash table structure used in dictionaries. This efficiency is especially valuable in applications that require quick lookups, such as caching mechanisms and database indexing.

**Intuitive Data Organization:** Key-value pairs provide a natural and intuitive way to organize data. This structure mimics real-world associations, making it easier for developers to model relationships between different data elements. For example, storing user information (e.g., usernames as keys and user details as values) is straightforward and easily understood.

**Flexibility:** Since values can be of any type, key-value pairs allow for a great deal of flexibility in data representation. You can store simple data types like integers and strings, as well as more complex structures like lists and nested dictionaries, enabling comprehensive data management.

**Dynamic Updates:** Key-value pairs in dictionaries can be easily updated, added, or deleted. This dynamic nature allows for efficient data management in applications that require frequent changes to the data structure.

### *Use Cases of Key-Value Pairs*

**Configuration Settings:** Applications often use key-value pairs to store configuration settings, where keys represent setting names (like "max_connections" or "timeout") and values hold their corresponding settings (like 100 or 30 seconds).

**Caching:** In caching mechanisms, key-value pairs are used to store frequently accessed data, allowing for rapid retrieval without repeated computation or database access.

**Data Serialization:** Key-value pairs are common in data serialization formats like JSON (JavaScript Object Notation), where they provide a simple way to represent structured data that can be easily transmitted over the web.

**Database Indexing:** Many database systems use key-value pair structures to index records, allowing for quick searches and efficient data retrieval.

## Creating and Accessing Dictionaries

Creating and accessing dictionaries in Python is straightforward and involves using a simple syntax. Here's a detailed explanation of how to create dictionaries, add or modify key-value pairs, and access the data stored in them.

### *Creating Dictionaries*

Using Curly Braces: The most common way to create a dictionary is by using curly braces {} with key-value pairs separated by colons:

***Here's an example:***

```
my_dict = {
    "name": "Alice",
    "age": 30,
    "city": "New York"
}
```

**Using the dict() Constructor:** You can also create a dictionary using the dict() constructor. This method allows you to pass key-value pairs as arguments:

```
my_dict = dict(name="Alice", age=30, city="New York")
```

**From a List of Tuples:** Another way to create a dictionary is by using a list of tuples, where each tuple contains a key-value pair:

```
my_dict = dict([("name", "Alice"), ("age", 30), ("city",
"New York")])
```

**Empty Dictionary:** You can start with an empty dictionary and add items later:

```
my_dict = {}
```

### *Accessing Dictionaries*

Once you have created a dictionary, you can easily access its elements using keys.

**Accessing Values:** To retrieve the value associated with a specific key, use the key inside square brackets []:

```
name = my_dict["name"]  # Retrieves the value associated
with the key "name"
print(name)  # Output: Alice
```

Using the get() Method: The get() method is another way to access values, and it provides a safer alternative to using square brackets. If the key does not exist, it returns None (or a specified default value) instead of raising a KeyError:

```
age = my_dict.get("age")  # Retrieves the value associated with the key "age"
print(age)  # Output: 30
# If the key does not exist
profession = my_dict.get("profession", "Not specified")  # Default value if key doesn't exist
print(profession)  # Output: Not specified
```

**Iterating Over Dictionaries:** You can iterate through keys, values, or key-value pairs using loops:

***Keys:***

```
for key in my_dict:
    print(key)  # Output: name, age, city
```

**Values:**

```
for value in my_dict.values():
    print(value)  # Output: Alice, 30, New York
```

**Key-Value Pairs:**

```
for key, value in my_dict.items():
  print(f"{key}: {value}")  # Output: name: Alice, age: 30, city: New York
```

***Modifying Dictionaries***

Adding Key-Value Pairs: To add a new key-value pair, simply assign a value to a new key:

```
my_dict["profession"] = "Engineer"
```

Updating Existing Values: You can update the value associated with an existing key in the same way:

```
my_dict["age"] = 31  # Update age from 30 to 31
```

Removing Key-Value Pairs: You can remove a key-value pair using the del statement or the pop() method:

```
del my_dict["city"]   # Removes the key "city" and its associated value
age = my_dict.pop("age")   # Removes the key "age" and returns its value
```

Creating and accessing dictionaries in Python is a fundamental skill for effective programming. Their flexible and efficient key-value pairing system allows for intuitive data management, making dictionaries an essential data structure in various applications, from simple scripts to complex data analysis. By mastering the creation, access, and modification of dictionaries, developers can better organize their data and enhance the functionality of their programs.

## Dictionary Operations

Dictionaries in Python support a range of operations that enable effective manipulation of key-value pairs. You can easily add items by assigning a value to a new key, update existing values, or remove items using methods like del or pop(). Checking for key existence is straightforward with the in keyword, while the clear() method can empty the dictionary entirely. These operations allow for dynamic data management, making dictionaries versatile for various programming tasks.

- Here are some fundamental operations:

Adding Items: In Python, adding new key-value pairs to a dictionary is straightforward and can be accomplished by simply assigning a value to a new key. If the key does not already exist in the dictionary, this operation creates a new entry.

***The syntax for adding an item is as follows:***

```
my_dict[key] = value
```

Here, key is the unique identifier for the value you want to store, and value can be of any data type, including strings, numbers, lists, or even other dictionaries.

***Example***

```
# Creating an initial dictionary
my_dict = {
    "name": "Alice",
    "age": 30
}
```

```
# Adding new key-value pairs
my_dict["city"] = "New York"   # Adds a new key 'city' with the value 'New York'
my_dict["profession"] = "Engineer"   # Adds a new key 'profession' with the value 'Engineer'

# The updated dictionary now contains the new entries
print(my_dict)
```

**Output**

```
{'name': 'Alice', 'age': 30, 'city': 'New York', 'profession': 'Engineer'}
```

In this example, two new key-value pairs are added to the my_dict dictionary, illustrating how easily you can expand your data structure to include additional information. If you try to add a key that already exists, Python will simply update the value associated with that key:

```
# Updating an existing key
my_dict["age"] = 31  # Changes the value of 'age' from 30 to 31

# The updated dictionary reflects the change
print(my_dict)
```

**Output**

```
{'name': 'Alice', 'age': 31, 'city': 'New York', 'profession': 'Engineer'}
```

This flexibility in adding and updating key-value pairs makes dictionaries a powerful tool for organizing data in Python.

**Updating Items:** In Python, updating the value associated with an existing key in a dictionary is a simple process that involves reassigning a new value to that key. This operation effectively replaces the old value with the new one while retaining the key itself. The syntax for updating an item is as follows:

```
my_dict[key] = new_value
```

Here, key is the existing key for which you want to update the value, and new_value is the new value you want to assign.

### *Example*

Here's a practical example to illustrate updating items in a dictionary:

```
# Creating an initial dictionary
my_dict = {
    "name": "Alice",
    "age": 30,
    "city": "New York"
}

# Updating the value associated with an existing key
my_dict["age"] = 31  # Changes the age from 30 to 31
my_dict["city"] = "San Francisco"  # Updates the city from
'New York' to 'San Francisco'

# The updated dictionary reflects the changes
print(my_dict)
```

**Output**

```
{'name': 'Alice', 'age': 31, 'city': 'San Francisco'}
```

In this example, the values for the keys "age" and "city" are updated. After the reassignment, the dictionary now reflects these new values while retaining the same keys.

### *Updating Multiple Keys*

You can also update multiple keys in one go using the update() method, which allows you to provide another dictionary or an iterable of key-value pairs:

```
# Updating multiple keys at once
my_dict.update({"age": 32, "profession": "Engineer"})  #
Changes age to 32 and adds 'profession'

# The updated dictionary reflects the changes
print(my_dict)
```

## Output

```
{'name': 'Alice', 'age': 32, 'city': 'San Francisco',
'profession': 'Engineer'}
```

This method is particularly useful when you need to make several updates simultaneously, enhancing the efficiency and readability of your code. Overall, the ability to update values easily makes dictionaries a highly flexible and powerful data structure in Python.

**Removing Items:** In Python, you can remove key-value pairs from a dictionary using either the del statement or the pop() method. The del statement allows you to delete a specific key and its associated value by specifying the key in the format del my_dict[key], which raises a KeyError if the key does not exist. Alternatively, the pop() method removes a key and returns its value, allowing for safe removal since you can provide a default return value to avoid errors if the key is not found (e.g., my_dict.pop(key, default)). Both methods are effective for managing dictionary contents, enabling you to dynamically modify your data structures as needed.

***Example:***

```
my_dict = {"name": "Alice", "age": 30}
del my_dict["age"]  # Removes the key 'age'
profession = my_dict.pop("profession", "Not found")  # Tries to remove 'profession' and returns 'Not found' if it doesn't exist
```

**Checking for Existence:** In Python, you can check for the existence of a key in a dictionary using the in keyword, which provides a straightforward way to determine whether a specific key is present. The syntax is simple and involves placing the key on the left side of the in keyword and the dictionary on the right side, like this:

```
key in my_dict
```

This expression evaluates to True if the key exists in the dictionary and False if it does not. This feature is particularly useful for avoiding errors when attempting to access or manipulate values associated with keys that may not be present.

***Example:***

Here's a practical example to illustrate how to check for key existence:

```
# Creating a dictionary
my_dict = {
    "name": "Alice",
    "age": 30,
    "city": "New York"
}

# Checking if a key exists
if "name" in my_dict:
    print("Key 'name' exists in the dictionary.")

if "profession" not in my_dict:
  print("Key 'profession' does not exist in the dictionary.")
```

**Output**

```
Key 'name' exists in the dictionary.
Key 'profession' does not exist in the dictionary.
```

In this example, the in keyword is used to check for the existence of the keys "name" and "profession" in my_dict. This allows you to safely perform operations like updating or deleting key-value pairs, ensuring that your code can handle situations where certain keys may be missing without raising errors. Overall, using the in keyword is an efficient way to manage dictionary data and validate key presence.

**Clearing the Dictionary:** In Python, the clear() method is used to remove all items from a dictionary, effectively emptying it while maintaining its structure as a dictionary object. When you call my_dict.clear(), all key-value pairs are deleted, and the dictionary becomes empty, with a length of zero. This method is particularly useful when you need to reset a dictionary for reuse without deleting the variable itself.

***Example***

Here's a practical example demonstrating how to use the clear() method:

```
# Creating a dictionary with some items
my_dict = {
    "name": "Alice",
    "age": 30,
    "city": "New York"
}

# Clearing the dictionary
my_dict.clear()

# Checking the contents of the dictionary after clearing
print(my_dict)  # Outputs: {}
```

**Output**

```
{}
```

In this example, after invoking my_dict.clear(), all entries in the dictionary are removed, resulting in an empty dictionary. It's important to note that while the clear() method deletes all items, the dictionary itself still exists and can be used to store new key-value pairs in the future. This method is a clean and efficient way to reset a dictionary when needed.

## Dictionary Methods

Python dictionaries come with a variety of built-in methods that enhance their usability. Here are some commonly used methods:

get(key, default=None): Returns the value for the specified key. If the key does not exist, it returns the specified default value (or None if no default is provided).

```
value = my_dict.get("name", "Unknown")  # Returns "Alice"
or "Unknown" if not found
```

**keys():** Returns a view object that displays a list of all the keys in the dictionary.

```
keys = my_dict.keys()  # Returns dict_keys(['name'])
```

**values():** Returns a view object that displays a list of all the values in the dictionary.

```
values = my_dict.values()  # Returns dict_values(['Alice'])
```

**items():** Returns a view object that displays a list of the dictionary's key-value pairs as tuples.

```
items = my_dict.items()   # Returns dict_items([('name', 'Alice')])
```

**pop(key, default=None):** Removes the specified key and returns its value. If the key does not exist, it returns the specified default value (or raises a KeyError if no default is provided).

```
age = my_dict.pop("age", "Not found")  # Removes "age" and returns its value or "Not found"
```

**update(other):** Updates the dictionary with key-value pairs from another dictionary or iterable of key-value pairs. If a key already exists, its value is updated.

```
my_dict.update({"age": 31, "city": "New York"})  # Updates or adds new pairs
```

**setdefault(key, default=None):** Returns the value of the specified key. If the key does not exist, it inserts the key with a specified default value.

```
my_dict.setdefault("profession", "Engineer")  # Adds "profession" with default "Engineer" if not present
```

## Dictionary Comprehension

Dictionary comprehension is a concise and efficient way to create dictionaries in Python. It allows you to construct a dictionary in a single line of code using a syntax similar to list comprehension.

The general syntax is as follows:

```
{key_expression: value_expression for item in iterable if condition}
```

### *Example 1: Simple Dictionary Comprehension*

You can create a dictionary from a list of keys and assign them all the same value:

```
keys = ['a', 'b', 'c']
my_dict = {key: 0 for key in keys}  # Creates {'a': 0, 'b': 0, 'c': 0}
```

***Example 2: Transforming Existing Data***

You can also use dictionary comprehension to transform data from an existing iterable. For instance, creating a dictionary that maps numbers to their squares:

```
squares = {x: x**2 for x in range(5)}  # Creates {0: 0, 1:
1, 2: 4, 3: 9, 4: 16}
```

***Example 3: Filtering Data***

You can include conditions to filter items while creating the dictionary:

```
even_squares = {x: x**2 for x in range(10) if x % 2 == 0}
# Creates {0: 0, 2: 4, 4: 16, 6: 36, 8: 64}
```

Understanding dictionary operations, methods, and comprehension in Python is essential for effective data manipulation and storage. The versatility and efficiency of dictionaries make them a powerful tool in a programmer's toolkit, enabling complex data organization and retrieval with minimal code. With these concepts, you can harness the full potential of dictionaries in your Python projects.

## Summary

Sets in Python are unordered collections of unique elements, meaning they do not allow duplicates. Sets can be created using curly braces {} or the set() function. They support a variety of operations such as union, intersection, difference, and symmetric difference. Set methods like add(), remove(), discard(), and clear() allow for easy manipulation of elements. Sets are highly efficient for membership tests and eliminating duplicates from other collections. Dictionaries, on the other hand, are unordered collections of key-value pairs, where each key is unique and maps to a specific value. Keys in dictionaries must be immutable types, and values can be of any data type. Dictionaries can be created using curly braces {} or the dict() function. Common dictionary methods include get(), items(), keys(), and values(). Dictionary comprehension offers a concise way to create dictionaries by specifying key-value pairs in a single line of code, similar to list comprehension. Both sets and dictionaries can be iterated over, with sets offering iteration through their elements and dictionaries through their keys or key-value pairs.

## Exercise Questions

- Create a set containing five unique numbers. Add two more numbers and print the updated set.
- Remove an element from a set using the remove() method and print the result.
- Create two sets and perform a union operation to combine them.

- Perform an intersection operation on two sets and print the result.
- Use the difference() method to find elements in one set that are not in another.
- Create a dictionary with at least three key-value pairs and print it.
- Access a value in a dictionary using a key and print it.
- Use the get() method to retrieve the value associated with a key in a dictionary.
- Add a new key-value pair to an existing dictionary and print the updated dictionary.
- Write a Python program to iterate over a dictionary and print each key-value pair.
- Create a nested dictionary and access a value inside the nested dictionary.
- Perform a dictionary comprehension to create a dictionary where the keys are numbers from 1 to 5 and the values are their squares.
- Write a Python program to check if a key exists in a dictionary using the in operator.
- Create two dictionaries and perform a merge operation to combine them.
- Write a Python program to demonstrate the use of clear() to remove all elements from a dictionary.

CHAPTER - 5

# Functions and Error Handling in Python

Functions and error handling are essential components of Python programming, enhancing code reusability and robustness. Functions are blocks of reusable code that perform specific tasks, defined using the def keyword followed by the function name and parameters (if any). Functions allow developers to organize code into logical sections, making it more readable and efficient. Error handling involves managing potential runtime errors to prevent program crashes and ensure smooth operation. Python uses the try, except, else, and finally blocks to catch and handle errors gracefully. The try block encloses code that might raise an exception, while the except block defines the response to specific exceptions. The else block executes if no errors occur, and finally contains code that runs regardless of any exceptions. Together, functions and error handling enable cleaner, more controlled code execution and error management.

## Functions

### Defining Function

In Python, a function is defined using the def keyword, followed by a function name, parentheses (), and a colon :. Inside the parentheses, you can specify parameters that act as placeholders for the arguments passed when the function is called. The function's code block, or "body," is indented beneath the definition line and contains the statements that will be executed when the function is invoked. A function can optionally return a value using the return statement.

***Syntax:***

```
def function_name(parameters):
    # Code block (function body)
    # Optional: return value
```

### *Example of a Function Definition:*

```
def greet(name):
    print(f"Hello, {name}!")
```

**In this example:**

- def starts the function definition.
- greet is the name of the function.
- name is a parameter, which means the function expects an argument to replace name when called.
- The function prints a greeting message using the argument provided.

You can call this function as follows:

```
greet("Alice")  # Output: Hello, Alice!
```

Defining a function allows you to organize code into reusable blocks, improving readability and efficiency. Functions can take inputs (parameters) and can optionally produce outputs (return statement), making them highly flexible for various tasks.

## Calling Function

After defining a function, you can call (or invoke) it to execute the code inside its body. When calling a function, you use its name followed by parentheses. If the function has parameters, you pass arguments into the parentheses to replace those parameters. Function calls allow you to reuse code, pass different values to work with, and get results from functions.

### *Basic Syntax for Calling a Function*

The syntax for calling a function is straightforward:

```
function_name(arguments)
```

**Here:**

- function_name is the name of the function you defined.
- arguments are the values you pass to the function's parameters.

### *Example of Calling a Function without Parameters*

If a function has no parameters, you simply call it with empty parentheses:

```
def greet():
    print("Hello, welcome to Python!")


# Calling the function
greet()  # Output: Hello, welcome to Python!
```

### *Example of Calling a Function with Parameters*

When a function has parameters, you need to provide arguments that correspond to each parameter:

```
def greet_user(name):
    print(f"Hello, {name}!")
# Calling the function with an argument
greet_user("Alice")  # Output: Hello, Alice!
```

In this example, "Alice" is the argument passed to the name parameter.

### *Types of Arguments in Function Calls*

Python supports various types of arguments in function calls, which provide flexibility in how functions receive inputs:

#### Positional Arguments:

Positional arguments are the most common type of arguments in Python functions. When calling a function, each argument you provide is assigned to the corresponding parameter based on its position in the function definition. This means the first argument goes to the first parameter, the second to the second, and so on. Positional arguments are straightforward to use and allow functions to receive values in a clear, ordered way. For example, in a function def add(a, b):, if you call add(3, 5), the value 3 will be assigned to a and 5 to b, following their order in the function call.

```
def add(a, b):
  return a + b
result = add(3, 5)  # Here, 3 is assigned to `a` and 5 to `b`
print(result)  # Output: 8
```

#### Keyword Arguments:

Keyword arguments allow you to pass values to function parameters by explicitly specifying each parameter's name, making the code more readable and flexible. This approach removes the reliance on argument order, as you can specify arguments in any order when calling the function. For instance, if a function is defined as def introduce(name, age):, you can call it with introduce(name="Alice", age=25) or even swap the order with introduce(age=25, name="Alice"). Using keyword arguments helps clarify which values correspond to which parameters, making the code self-explanatory and reducing the likelihood of errors.

```
def introduce(name, age):
    print(f"My name is {name} and I am {age} years old.")
introduce(name="Alice", age=25)
introduce(age=30, name="Bob")  # Order doesn't matter with keywords
```

**Default Arguments:**

If a function has parameters with default values, you can skip passing arguments for those parameters when calling the function, and Python will automatically use the default values specified. This feature is helpful for creating flexible functions that can be called with or without certain arguments. For instance, if a function is defined as def greet_user(name="Guest"), calling greet_user("Alice") will print "Hello, Alice!" because "Alice" replaces the default value. However, if you call greet_user() without any argument, it will output "Hello, Guest!" since the default "Guest" is used. Default parameters simplify function calls and make functions adaptable to various scenarios.

```
def greet_user(name="Guest"):
    print(f"Hello, {name}!")

greet_user("Alice")  # Output: Hello, Alice!
greet_user()         # Output: Hello, Guest!
```

**Variable-Length Arguments:**

Sometimes, you don't know how many arguments will be passed. In these cases, Python allows you to use *args for a variable number of positional arguments or **kwargs for a variable number of keyword arguments.

```
# *args example
def add_all(*numbers):
    return sum(numbers)

print(add_all(1, 2, 3, 4))  # Output: 10
```

```
# **kwargs example
def print_info(**info):
    for key, value in info.items():
        print(f"{key}: {value}")

print_info(name="Alice", age=25, city="New York")
```

### Nested Function Calls

In Python, you can call one function inside another function, which allows you to build complex operations by combining simpler tasks. For instance, if you have an add function that sums two numbers, you could call it within another function square_sum to first add the numbers and then square the result. This promotes modular code and reduces redundancy by reusing existing functions.Also, Python allows functions to call themselves within their own body, a concept known as recursion. Recursive functions are useful for tasks that can be broken down into smaller sub-tasks of the same type, such as calculating factorials or performing search operations in data structures. For example, a recursive function to calculate the factorial of a number n might look like def factorial(n): return 1 if n == 0 else n * factorial(n - 1). Here, factorial calls itself until it reaches the base case (when n equals 0). Recursion enables elegant solutions for problems with repetitive or self-similar structures but should be used carefully to avoid excessive memory use and infinite loops.

***Here's a simple example:***

```
def add(a, b):
    return a + b
def square_sum(a, b):
    result = add(a, b)
    return result * result

print(square_sum(3, 4))  # Output: 49, as (3+4)^2 = 49
```

## Calling a Function with Return Values

When calling a function that returns a value, you can store the result in a variable or use it directly.

```
def multiply(a, b):
    return a * b

# Calling the function and storing the result
result = multiply(5, 3)
print(result)  # Output: 15

# Using the return value directly
print(multiply(4, 7))  # Output: 28
```

Calling a function in Python is a straightforward process that activates the code in its body. You call a function by using its name and providing any required arguments based on its parameters. The different types of arguments (positional, keyword, default, and variable-length) give you flexibility in how you pass data. By calling functions, you can reuse code, simplify complex tasks, and structure the program in a way that is easier to read and maintain.

## Parameters and Arguments

In Python, parameters and arguments are essential concepts in functions that define how data is passed to and processed by a function.Parameters are the variables specified within the parentheses in a function definition. They act as placeholders for values that will be passed to the function. For example, in def greet(name):, name is a parameter. Parameters define what inputs the function expects but do not have actual values until the function is called.Arguments are the actual values you pass to a function when you call it. These values replace the parameters within the function, allowing the function to operate with specific data. For instance, in the function call greet("Alice"), "Alice" is an argument that takes the place of name in the function, allowing greet to print a personalized message.In short, parameters are the placeholders defined in the function header, while arguments are the actual values provided when calling the function. Understanding the distinction between parameters and arguments helps in effectively designing and calling functions.

Here's a simple example of how a table can be formatted to explain the concepts of parameters and arguments in a function (Table 5.1).

**Table 5.1: Concepts of Parameters and Arguments in a Function**

| Term | Definition | Example in Function Definition | Example in Function Call |
|---|---|---|---|
| Parameters | Placeholders defined in the function header, specifying what inputs the function will expect. | def greet(name): (Here, name is a parameter) | N/A |

| | | | |
|---|---|---|---|
| Arguments | Actual values passed to the function when it's called, replacing the parameters within the function. | N/A | greet("Alice") (Here, "Alice" is an argument) |

## Docstrings

Docstrings in Python are string literals that appear as the first statement in a function, method, class, or module definition. They serve as documentation for the code, providing a convenient way to explain what the function or module does, what parameters it takes, and what it returns. Docstrings are enclosed in triple quotes (""" or '''), allowing them to span multiple lines if necessary.

### *Purpose of Docstrings*

**Documentation:** They provide clarity on how to use the function or module, making it easier for others (and yourself) to understand the code later.

**Help Function:** They can be accessed using the built-in help() function, which displays the documentation for that function, aiding users in understanding its usage without needing to read through the entire code.

### *Example of a Function with a Docstring*

Here's how you can define a function with a docstring:

```
def add(a, b):
    """
    Add two numbers and return the result.

    Parameters:
    a (int or float): The first number to be added.
    b (int or float): The second number to be added.

    Returns:
    int or float: The sum of a and b.
    """
    return a + b
```

**In this example:**

The docstring describes what the function does (adding two numbers), specifies the parameters it accepts (a and b), and indicates the return value.The format used in the docstring is common practice and can be further enhanced with specific conventions like NumPy or Google style for consistency and clarity.

### *Accessing Docstrings*

You can access the docstring of a function using the __doc__ attribute or the help() function:

```
print(add.__doc__)
# or
help(add)
```

This output will show the documentation provided in the docstring, making it a valuable resource for users and developers to understand how to utilize the function effectively.

Docstrings are an essential part of writing clear and maintainable code in Python. They allow developers to document their code succinctly and accessibly, facilitating better understanding and collaboration. Writing informative docstrings is considered good practice in Python programming.

## Lambda Functions

Lambda functions in Python are small, anonymous functions defined using the lambda keyword. Unlike regular functions defined with the def keyword, lambda functions are typically used for short, throwaway functions that are not bound to a name. They can take any number of parameters but can only have a single expression, which makes them concise and useful for specific tasks, especially when passing functions as arguments to higher-order functions.

### *Syntax of Lambda Functions*

The syntax for a lambda function is:

```
lambda arguments: expression
```

- lambda is the keyword that defines the function.
- arguments are the parameters that the function can take.
- expression is the single expression that is evaluated and returned when the function is called.

### *Example of a Lambda Function*

Here's a simple example of a lambda function that adds two numbers:

```
add = lambda x, y: x + y
result = add(3, 5)
print(result)  # Output: 8
```

In this example, the lambda function takes two arguments, x and y, and returns their sum. The function is assigned to the variable add, which can then be called like a regular function.

### *Use Cases for Lambda Functions*

**Inline Functions:** Lambda functions are often used where small functions are required for a short period, such as in the map(), filter(), and reduce() functions.

**Using map():** Apply a function to all items in a list.

```
numbers = [1, 2, 3, 4]
squares = list(map(lambda x: x ** 2, numbers))
print(squares)  # Output: [1, 4, 9, 16]
```

**Using filter():** Filter elements from a list based on a condition.

```
evens = list(filter(lambda x: x % 2 == 0, numbers))
print(evens)  # Output: [2, 4]
```

**Sorting with Custom Keys:** Lambda functions can be used as a custom key for sorting.

```
points = [(2, 3), (1, 5), (4, 1)]
sorted_points = sorted(points, key=lambda point: point[1])
print(sorted_points)  # Output: [(4, 1), (2, 3), (1, 5)]
```

**Returning Functions:** Lambda functions can be returned from other functions.

```
def make_incrementer(n):
    return lambda x: x + n
increment_by_2 = make_incrementer(2)
print(increment_by_2(5))  # Output: 7
```

### *Limitations of Lambda Functions*

While lambda functions are powerful, they have limitations:

**Single Expression:** They can only contain a single expression, which limits their complexity. You cannot include statements or multiple expressions.

**Readability:** Overusing lambda functions can make code less readable, especially if the function logic is complex. In such cases, defining a regular function with def is preferable.

## Using Lambdas with Map

Using lambda functions with the map() function in Python allows you to apply a function to every item in an iterable (such as a list or a tuple) and create a new iterable with the results. The map() function takes two main arguments: a function (which can be a lambda function) and an iterable. It applies the function to each item in the iterable, returning a map object that can be converted to a list or other collection types.

### *Syntax of map()*

The syntax for using map() with a lambda function is:

```
map(function, iterable)
```

### *Example of Using Lambda with map()*

Here's a simple example to illustrate how to use lambda functions with map():

### Example 1: Squaring Numbers

Suppose you have a list of numbers and want to create a new list containing the squares of those numbers:

```
numbers = [1, 2, 3, 4, 5]
squared = list(map(lambda x: x ** 2, numbers))
print(squared)  # Output: [1, 4, 9, 16, 25]
```

**In this example:**

- The lambda function lambda x: x ** 2 squares each number in the numbers list.
- The map() function applies this lambda to each element of numbers.
- The result is converted to a list, yielding [1, 4, 9, 16, 25].

### Example 2: Converting Temperatures

You can also use map() with lambda functions to convert temperatures from Celsius to Fahrenheit:

```
celsius = [0, 20, 37, 100]
fahrenheit = list(map(lambda c: (c * 9/5) + 32, celsius))
print(fahrenheit)  # Output: [32.0, 68.0, 98.6, 212.0]
```

**Here:**

- The lambda function lambda c: (c * 9/5) + 32 converts Celsius to Fahrenheit.
- The map() function applies this conversion to each value in the celsius list, resulting in the fahrenheit list.

***Example 3: Using Multiple Iterables***

You can also use map() with multiple iterables. For instance, if you want to add corresponding elements from two lists:

```
list1 = [1, 2, 3]
list2 = [4, 5, 6]
result = list(map(lambda x, y: x + y, list1, list2))
print(result)  # Output: [5, 7, 9]
```

**In this case:**

- The lambda function takes two parameters x and y and returns their sum.
- The map() function combines the corresponding elements from list1 and list2.

## Filter and Reduce Functions

The filter() and reduce() functions in Python are higher-order functions that facilitate functional programming by allowing you to apply functions to iterables. While filter() is used to filter elements from an iterable based on a condition, reduce() is used to cumulatively apply a function to the items of an iterable, reducing it to a single value.

### 1. Filter Function

filter() is used to create a subset of an iterable, retaining only those elements for which a given function returns True. It takes two arguments: a function (often a lambda function) and an iterable.

***Syntax***

```
filter(function, iterable)
```

**function:** A function that tests whether each element of the iterable is True or False. If it returns True, the element is included in the result.

**iterable:** The iterable (like a list, tuple, etc.) to be filtered.

### *Example of Using filter()*

Here's an example that filters out even numbers from a list:

```
numbers = [1, 2, 3, 4, 5, 6]
odd_numbers = list(filter(lambda x: x % 2 != 0, numbers))
print(odd_numbers)  # Output: [1, 3, 5]
```

**In this example:**

- The lambda function checks if a number is odd.
- The filter() function applies this check to each number in the numbers list, returning only the odd numbers.

### 2. Reduce Function

reduce() is used to apply a function cumulatively to the items of an iterable, reducing it to a single accumulated result. This function is part of the functools module, so you need to import it before using it.

#### *Syntax*

```
from functools import reduce
reduce(function, iterable[, initializer])
```

- function: A function of two arguments that is applied cumulatively to the items of the iterable.
- iterable: The iterable whose items are to be reduced.
- initializer (optional): A value that is used as the initial accumulator.

### *Example of Using reduce()*

Here's an example that multiplies all numbers in a list:

```
from functools import reduce
numbers = [1, 2, 3, 4]
product = reduce(lambda x, y: x * y, numbers)
print(product)  # Output: 24
```

**In this example:**

- The lambda function takes two arguments x and y and returns their product.
- The reduce() function applies this multiplication cumulatively across the numbers list, resulting in the final product of 24.

***Example of Using reduce() with an Initializer***

You can also use an initializer with reduce(), which acts as the starting point for the accumulation:

- numbers = [1, 2, 3, 4]
- sum_with_initializer = reduce(lambda x, y: x + y, numbers, 10)
- print(sum_with_initializer) # Output: 20

**Here:**

The accumulation starts with the initializer value of 10, so the result is 10 + 1 + 2 + 3 + 4 = 20.

## Error Handling

Error handling in Python is a mechanism that allows programmers to manage exceptions—unexpected events that disrupt the normal flow of execution in a program. It enables developers to anticipate potential errors and define responses to those errors, thereby preventing crashes and improving the robustness of applications. Python provides several constructs for error handling, primarily through the use of try, except, else, and finally blocks. The try block contains code that might raise an exception, while the except block specifies how to handle the exception if it occurs. The else block can be used to define code that runs if the try block succeeds without raising an exception, and the finally block is executed regardless of whether an exception occurred, making it ideal for resource cleanup. By implementing error handling, developers can create more resilient applications that can gracefully recover from unexpected issues.

In Python, errors can be classified into several types, including syntax errors and exceptions. Understanding these errors, including built-in and user-defined exceptions, as well as how to handle them using the try, except, else, and finally constructs, is crucial for writing robust and error-tolerant code.

### 1. Syntax Errors

Syntax errors occur when the code violates the grammatical rules of Python, preventing the interpreter from parsing the code. These errors must be fixed before the program can run. Common causes of syntax errors include:

- Missing punctuation: Such as forgetting a colon at the end of a function definition or an if statement.
- Mismatched parentheses, brackets, or quotes: Not closing parentheses or using mismatched quotes will raise a syntax error.
- Improper indentation: Python uses indentation to define blocks of code, and incorrect indentation will lead to syntax errors.

***Example:***

```
def my_function()
  print("Hello, world!")  # Missing colon after function
definition
```

## 2. Exceptions

Exceptions are runtime errors that occur during program execution, indicating that something went wrong. Python has a rich set of built-in exceptions that cover a wide range of errors. Exceptions can be broadly categorized into:

### *Built-in Exceptions*

Python provides a variety of built-in exceptions that you can handle in your programs. Some common built-in exceptions include:

- ZeroDivisionError: Raised when trying to divide by zero.
- TypeError: Raised when an operation is applied to an inappropriate type.
- ValueError: Raised when a function receives an argument of the correct type but an inappropriate value.
- IndexError: Raised when trying to access an index that is out of range in a list or sequence.
- KeyError: Raised when trying to access a non-existent key in a dictionary.
- FileNotFoundError: Raised when trying to open a file that does not exist.

***Example of a built-in exception:***

```
x = 1 / 0  # Raises ZeroDivisionError
```

### User-Defined Exceptions

In addition to built-in exceptions, Python allows you to create your own custom exceptions by inheriting from the Exception class. This is useful when you want to signal specific error conditions that are relevant to your application.

***Example of a user-defined exception:***

```
class MyCustomError(Exception):
    pass

def my_function(value):
    if value < 0:
        raise MyCustomError("Value must be non-negative")
```

```
try:
    my_function(-1)
except MyCustomError as e:
    print(e)  # Output: Value must be non-negative
```

## 3. Exception Handling with try, except, else, and finally

Python provides a structured way to handle exceptions using the try and except blocks. Here's how they work:

- try block: Contains the code that may raise an exception.
- except block: Catches and handles the exception if one occurs. You can specify the type of exception you want to catch.
- else block: Executes if the code in the try block runs without raising any exceptions.
- finally block: Executes regardless of whether an exception occurred or not. It's typically used for cleanup actions (e.g., closing files).

**Example:**

```
try:
    result = 10 / 0  # This will raise ZeroDivisionError
except ZeroDivisionError:
    print("You cannot divide by zero!")
else:
    print("Division successful:", result)
finally:
    print("Execution complete.")
Output:
csharp
You cannot divide by zero!
Execution complete.
```

## 4. Raising Exceptions

You can raise exceptions intentionally in your code using the raise statement. This is useful when you want to enforce certain conditions or notify the caller of your function about an error.

***Example:***

```
def check_positive(number):
    if number < 0:
        raise ValueError("Number must be positive")
try:
    check_positive(-5)
except ValueError as e:
    print(e)  # Output: Number must be positive
```

## Summary

Functions and Error Handling in Python covers essential concepts for writing modular and robust code. It begins with functions, detailing how to define and call them, the importance of parameters and arguments, and the role of docstrings for documentation. The unit then introduces lambda functions, explaining their syntax and usage, as well as how they can be utilized with higher-order functions like map, filter, and reduce for efficient data processing. Furthermore, it delves into error handling by distinguishing between syntax errors and exceptions, including built-in and user-defined exceptions. The unit emphasizes the significance of exception handling using the try, except, else, and finally constructs to manage errors gracefully and ensure program reliability while also discussing how to raise exceptions deliberately when necessary.

## Exercise Questions

- Define a function called greet that takes a name as an argument and prints a greeting message. Call this function with your name as the argument.
- Write a function named calculate_area that takes the length and width of a rectangle as parameters and returns its area.
- Create a function is_even that takes an integer as an argument and returns True if the number is even, and False otherwise. Test the function with different integers.
- Write a function that accepts a list of numbers and returns the maximum value in that list.
- Define a function that calculates the factorial of a given number using recursion. Test your function with different values.
- Create a lambda function that squares a number and use it to print the squares of the numbers from 1 to 10.
- Use the map function with a lambda to convert a list of strings to uppercase.

- Write a function that uses the filter function to return only the odd numbers from a given list.
- Define a function that accepts a list of integers and returns a new list containing only the positive integers using list comprehension.
- Write a function that takes two arguments, a base and an exponent, and returns the result of raising the base to the exponent (without using the ** operator).
- Write a program that prompts the user for two numbers and divides them, handling any potential division by zero errors with appropriate error messages.
- Create a function get_number that continuously prompts the user for a number until they enter a valid integer. Handle any exceptions that occur.
- Define a custom exception called NegativeNumberError that is raised when a negative number is passed to a function. Create a function that raises this exception if the input is negative.
- Write a program that attempts to open a file that doesn't exist. Use a try block to handle the exception and print a user-friendly error message.
- Create a function that takes a list and an index as arguments, returning the element at that index. Use exception handling to manage IndexError.
- Implement a function that takes a string and attempts to convert it to an integer, handling any ValueError that might occur.
- Write a function that takes a dictionary and a key as parameters and returns the value associated with the key. Use exception handling to manage KeyError.
- Define a function that reads data from a file and returns its content, handling any potential file-related errors with appropriate messages.
- Create a program that demonstrates the use of else with a try block. Print a message if no exceptions occurred during execution.
- Write a function that raises an exception when a user tries to enter a number greater than 100 and handle that exception in your main program.

CHAPTER - 6

# Python Library & Pandas

## Python Libraries

Python libraries are collections of pre-written code that provide specific functionalities, making it easier for developers to implement complex tasks without starting from scratch. They cover a vast array of domains, including data analysis, machine learning, web development, scientific computing, and more. Popular libraries like NumPy and Pandas are widely used in data science, offering powerful tools for handling arrays, matrices, and data manipulation. Matplotlib and Seaborn provide visualization capabilities, enabling users to create informative and appealing graphs. Libraries such as Requests simplify HTTP requests, making it easier to interact with web APIs, while Beautiful Soup aids in web scraping, allowing for automated extraction of data from HTML and XML files.For machine learning and deep learning, libraries like Scikit-Learn, TensorFlow, and PyTorch are indispensable. Scikit-Learn offers tools for implementing classic machine learning algorithms, from regression to clustering, while TensorFlow and PyTorch support the creation of neural networks and are used heavily in artificial intelligence research and applications. Django and Flask are popular web development libraries that simplify backend development, helping developers build robust and scalable web applications. By leveraging these libraries, Python developers can save time and effort, enabling them to focus on higher-level aspects of programming and problem-solving.

## Numpy

NumPy (Numerical Python) is a powerful Python library primarily used for numerical and scientific computing. It provides an array object, ndarray, that allows for fast and efficient storage and manipulation of large datasets, especially useful for numerical operations. Unlike Python lists, NumPy arrays have fixed data types and dimensions, which enables much faster processing for operations like element-wise calculations, linear algebra, and matrix manipulation. It's especially valuable in fields like data science, machine learning, and engineering, where handling and analyzing large datasets is common.NumPy offers a wide range of mathematical functions, including trigonometric, statistical, and algebraic functions, that can be applied directly to arrays. This library also includes tools for generating random numbers, reshaping data, and broadcasting, which allows operations on arrays of different shapes. One of its key advantages is its compatibility with other scientific libraries like Pandas, SciPy, and Matplotlib, which rely on NumPy for efficient data handling. With its speed and versatility, NumPy serves as a foundation for data-driven tasks and is widely regarded as essential in the Python scientific computing ecosystem.

- *NumPy is an essential tool in Python for efficient numerical and scientific computing, offering a range of applications across various fields (Figure 6.1):*

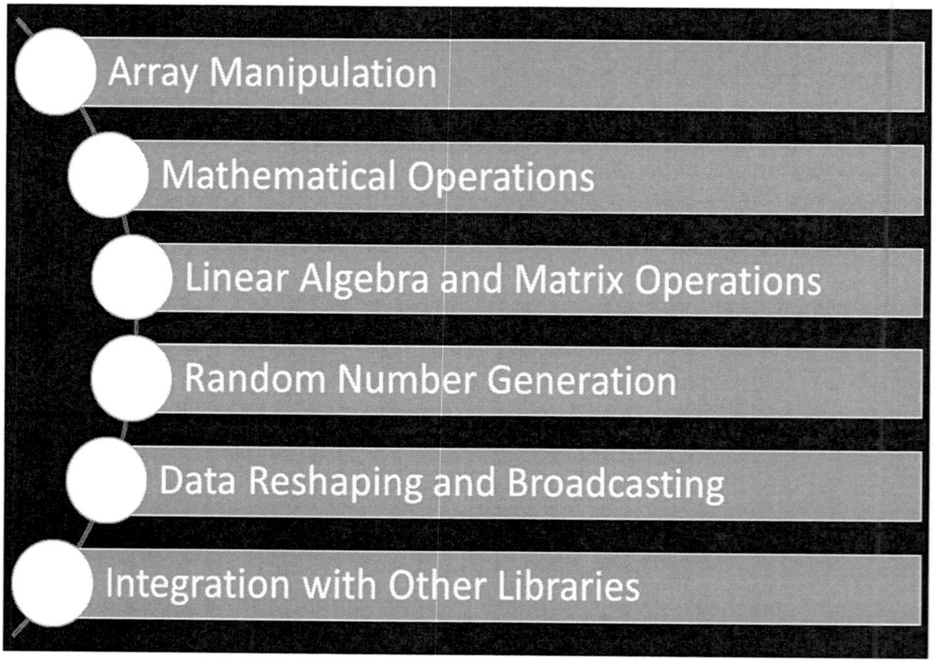


**Figure 6.1: Used of Numpy**

Array Manipulation: NumPy's core feature is its powerful ndarray object, which allows for creating and manipulating arrays (1D, 2D, or higher-dimensional). It supports fast element-wise operations, such as addition, subtraction, multiplication, and division, which are significantly faster than Python lists due to optimized memory handling and fixed data types.

**Mathematical Operations:** With its vast library of mathematical functions, NumPy makes it easy to perform complex operations like trigonometric calculations, exponential and logarithmic functions, and statistical operations directly on arrays. These functions are highly optimized for speed, making them ideal for heavy calculations.

**Linear Algebra and Matrix Operations:** NumPy provides a rich set of functions for linear algebra, such as matrix multiplication, transposition, inversion, eigenvalue computation, and more. This functionality is essential in data science and machine learning, where matrices and vectors are fundamental components.

**Random Number Generation:** NumPy includes a submodule, numpy.random, for generating random numbers, distributions, and sampling. This is highly useful in simulations, random sampling, probabilistic modeling, and initializing parameters in machine learning algorithms.

**Data Reshaping and Broadcasting:** NumPy enables reshaping arrays (e.g., converting a 1D array to 2D), splitting, stacking, and concatenating arrays. Broadcasting is another powerful feature, allowing operations on arrays of different shapes, making it easier to work with data of varying sizes without explicit loops.

**Integration with Other Libraries:** NumPy is foundational in the Python scientific stack, meaning it integrates seamlessly with libraries like Pandas for data analysis, Matplotlib for visualization, SciPy for scientific computing, and TensorFlow and PyTorch for machine learning. It's often used to preprocess data, handle large datasets, and create efficient data pipelines.

## Creating Numpy Array

Creating a NumPy array is fundamental to using the NumPy library for data manipulation and numerical computations. There are several ways to create arrays in NumPy, each suited to different scenarios. Here's a detailed look at these methods:

### 1. Creating Arrays from Python Lists or Tuples

One of the most common ways to create a NumPy array is by converting an existing list or tuple into an array using numpy.array().

```
import numpy as np
# From a list
array_from_list = np.array([1, 2, 3, 4])
print(array_from_list)  # Output: [1 2 3 4]
# From a tuple
array_from_tuple = np.array((5, 6, 7))
print(array_from_tuple)  # Output: [5 6 7]
```

### 2. Using Built-in Functions to Create Arrays with Specific Values

NumPy provides a variety of functions for creating arrays filled with specific values, shapes, or patterns:

**np.zeros():** Creates an array filled with zeros.

```
zeros_array = np.zeros((2, 3))  # 2×3 array of zeros
print(zeros_array)
# Output:
# [[0. 0. 0.]
#  [0. 0. 0.]]
```

**np.ones():** Creates an array filled with ones.

```
ones_array = np.ones((3, 2))  # 3×2 array of ones
print(ones_array)
```

**np.full():** Creates an array filled with a specified value.

```
full_array = np.full((2, 2), 7)  # 2×2 array filled with 7
print(full_array)
```

**np.eye():** Creates an identity matrix (square matrix with ones on the diagonal and zeros elsewhere).

```
identity_matrix = np.eye(3)  # 3×3 identity matrix
print(identity_matrix)
```

### 3. Creating Arrays with a Sequence of Numbers

To generate arrays with sequences, you can use functions like np.arange() and np.linspace().

**np.arange():** Creates an array with a specified range of values and an optional step.

```
sequence_array = np.arange(0, 10, 2)  # Start at 0, end before 10, step of 2
print(sequence_array)  # Output: [0 2 4 6 8]
```

**np.linspace():** Generates an array with evenly spaced values over a specified range.

```
linear_array = np.linspace(0, 1, 5)  # 5 evenly spaced values between 0 and 1
print(linear_array)  # Output: [0.   0.25 0.5  0.75 1. ]
```

### 4. Creating Random Arrays

NumPy's random module provides methods to create arrays filled with random values, which are useful for simulations, testing, and initializing machine learning models.

**np.random.rand():** Generates an array of random values between 0 and 1 with a specified shape.

```
random_array = np.random.rand(2, 3)  # 2×3 array with random
floats between 0 and 1
print(random_array)
```

**np.random.randint():** Generates an array of random integers within a specified range.

```
random_int_array = np.random.randint(1, 10, (2, 2))  # 2×2
array with random integers between 1 and 9
print(random_int_array)
```

### 5. Using Reshaping to Change Array Dimensions

Arrays can be reshaped to fit different dimensions. This can be done using the .reshape() method, which returns an array with the specified shape, as long as the total number of elements remains the same.

```
reshaped_array = np.arange(6).reshape((2, 3))  # Reshape a
1D array into 2×3
print(reshaped_array)
# Output:
# [[0 1 2]
#  [3 4 5]]
```

### 6. Creating Arrays with Empty or Uninitialized Values

If you want to create an array without initializing the values (useful for performance in certain cases), you can use np.empty().

```
empty_array = np.empty((2, 2)) # 2×2 array with uninitialized
values
print(empty_array)
```

Table brief different methods for creating NumPy arrays in Python:

**Table 6.1: Methods for Creating Numpy Arrays**

| Method | Function | Description | Example |
|---|---|---|---|
| **From List/ Tuple** | np.array() | Converts a list or tuple to a NumPy array. | np.array([1, 2, 3]) → [1 2 3] |
| **Array of Zeros** | np.zeros() | Creates an array filled with zeros, with specified shape. | np.zeros((2, 3)) → [[0. 0. 0.] [0. 0. 0.]] |
| **Array of Ones** | np.ones() | Creates an array filled with ones, with specified shape. | np.ones((2, 3)) → [[1. 1. 1.] [1. 1. 1.]] |
| **Constant Array** | np.full() | Creates an array filled with a specified constant. | np.full((2, 2), 7) → [[7 7] [7 7]] |
| **Identity Matrix** | np.eye() | Creates an identity matrix (1's on diagonal, 0's elsewhere). | np.eye(3) → [[1. 0. 0.] [0. 1. 0.] [0. 0. 1.]] |
| **Sequence Array** | np.arange() | Creates an array with a sequence of numbers (like range but returns an array). | np.arange(0, 10, 2) → [0 2 4 6 8] |
| **Linearly Spaced** | np.linspace() | Generates evenly spaced values between a start and end, with a specified count. | np.linspace(0, 1, 5) → [0. 0.25 0.5 0.75 1. ] |
| **Random Floats** | np.random.rand() | Creates an array with random float values between 0 and 1, with specified shape. | np.random.rand(2, 3) → [[0.1 0.2 0.3] [0.4 0.5 0.6]] (values will vary) |
| Random Integers | np.random.randint() | Creates an array with random integer values within a specified range and shape. | np.random.randint(1, 10, (2, 2)) → [[2 7] [5 3]] (values will vary) |
| **Uninitialized** | np.empty() | Creates an array with uninitialized values (can be faster but values are unpredictable). | np.empty((2, 2)) → [[1.3e-10 5.0e-324] [2.5e-323 1.0e-322]] (values will vary) |
| **Reshaped Array** | .reshape() | Reshapes an existing array to a specified new shape, without changing its data. | np.arange(6).reshape((2, 3)) → [[0 1 2] [3 4 5]] |

This table provides a quick reference for each method, including examples to demonstrate their use in creating arrays with NumPy (Table 6.1).

## Mathematical operations on Numpy

NumPy provides a rich set of mathematical operations for performing calculations on arrays, enabling efficient and expressive code for scientific and analytical computing. These operations include basic element-wise arithmetic, aggregate functions, trigonometric and exponential calculations, matrix manipulations, and statistical measures.

- Here's a detailed overview of the main categories and functionalities:

### 1. Basic Arithmetic Operations

NumPy allows basic arithmetic to be performed directly between arrays or between an array and a scalar:

- Addition, Subtraction, Multiplication, Division: Using operators like +, -, *, /, these operations are applied element-wise.
- Power and Modulus: ** and % enable element-wise exponentiation and modulus, respectively.
- Broadcasting: Allows operations between arrays of different shapes, where NumPy automatically stretches dimensions to match compatible shapes.

***Example:***

```
a = np.array([1, 2, 3])
b = np.array([4, 5, 6])
print(a + b)  # Output: [5 7 9]
print(a * 2)  # Output: [2 4 6]
```

- 2. Aggregate Functions
- Aggregate functions provide a summary of the data:
- Sum, Product, Mean: np.sum(), np.prod(), and np.mean() return the sum, product, and mean of elements in an array.
- Max, Min: np.max() and np.min() return the maximum and minimum values.
- Axis-specific Aggregates: These functions support an axis parameter, allowing operations along rows or columns in a 2D array.

***Example:***

```
c = np.array([[1, 2], [3, 4]])
print(np.sum(c, axis=0))  # Sum along columns: [4 6]
print(np.mean(c, axis=1)) # Mean along rows: [1.5 3.5]
```

### 3. Exponential and Logarithmic Functions

NumPy includes functions for advanced mathematical calculations:

**Exponential and Logarithmic Calculations:** np.exp() computes $e^x$ for each element, while np.log() and np.log10() compute the natural and base-10 logarithms.

**Logarithm Specialization:** This is useful in scientific fields where exponential growth models and scaling are common.

***Example:***

```
x = np.array([1, 10, 100])
print(np.log(x))  # Output: [0. 2.302 4.605]
```

### 4. Trigonometric Functions

- NumPy provides functions for sine, cosine, tangent, and their inverses, operating element-wise:
- Trigonometric Functions: np.sin(), np.cos(), np.tan() take inputs in radians, returning the respective trigonometric values.
- Inverse Trigonometric Functions: Functions like np.arcsin() return the angle in radians for a given sine value.

***Example:***

```
angles = np.array([0, np.pi/2, np.pi])
print(np.sin(angles))  # Output: [0. 1. 0.]
```

### 5. Rounding Operations

NumPy offers rounding functions for fine control over numerical precision:

- Rounding: np.round() rounds to a specified number of decimals.
- Floor and Ceiling: np.floor() rounds down to the nearest integer, while np.ceil() rounds up.

***Example:***

```
values = np.array([1.3, 2.7, -1.2])
print(np.floor(values))   # Output: [1. 2. -2.]
```

### 6. Matrix Multiplication and Linear Algebra Operations

- NumPy provides specialized functions for linear algebra:

- Dot Product and Matrix Multiplication: np.dot() and the @ operator allow matrix and vector dot products.
- Matrix Inversion, Determinant, Eigenvalues: np.linalg.inv(), np.linalg.det(), np.linalg.eig() are used for inverting matrices, calculating determinants, and finding eigenvalues.

***Example:***

```
A = np.array([[1, 2], [3, 4]])
B = np.array([[5, 6], [7, 8]])
print(A @ B)  # Output: [[19 22] [43 50]]
```

### 7. Comparison and Logical Operations

Logical and comparison operators apply element-wise to arrays:

- Comparison Operators: Operators like >, <, and == compare elements, returning boolean arrays.
- Logical Operations: np.all() checks if all elements meet a condition, while np.any() checks if any element does.

***Example:***

```
arr = np.array([1, 2, 3])
print(arr > 2)  # Output: [False False True]
```

### 8. Statistical Operations

Statistical operations allow for data analysis:

- Standard Deviation and Variance: np.std() and np.var() compute the spread of values.
- Median: np.median() provides the middle value, useful in data science and finance.

***Example:***

```
data = np.array([1, 2, 3, 4])
print(np.std(data))  # Output: 1.11803398875
```

These operations make NumPy a powerful tool for working with large datasets and performing complex numerical computations efficiently, which is especially beneficial in data science, machine learning, and scientific computing.

## Slicing and Indexing in numpy Arrays

Slicing and indexing in NumPy arrays are essential for accessing specific elements, rows, columns, or subarrays, offering versatility in data manipulation. Indexing is straightforward in 1D arrays, where each element can be accessed using a single index. For example, if arr = np.array([10, 20, 30, 40]), arr[2] will return 30. In 2D arrays, indexing involves specifying row and column positions. Given an array arr = np.array([[1, 2, 3], [4, 5, 6], [7, 8, 9]]), accessing arr[1, 2] would yield 6, targeting the element in the second row and third column. Multi-dimensional arrays allow similar indexing, with additional indices for each extra dimension. This method gives precise control over individual elements in complex datasets. Slicing extends this control, enabling access to a range of elements. In 1D arrays, slicing is done using a colon syntax, where arr[start:end] extracts elements from start up to but not including end. For example, arr[1:3] on [10, 20, 30, 40] would yield [20, 30]. In multi-dimensional arrays, slicing lets you work with entire rows or columns by leaving other indices blank. For instance, arr[:, 1:3] extracts columns two and three from all rows in a 2D array. Advanced slicing techniques, such as setting step values (e.g., arr[::2] to select every second element), or combining slices across dimensions, enhance flexibility. These tools allow easy extraction, manipulation, and analysis of array sections, crucial for effective data analysis and scientific computing.

### 1. Indexing in NumPy Arrays

- Basic Indexing: In a 1D array, indexing works similarly to lists, using zero-based indices. For example, arr[0] accesses the first element.
- Multi-dimensional Indexing: For 2D or higher-dimensional arrays, you use a comma-separated format to access elements. For example, arr[2, 3] accesses the element in the 3rd row and 4th column in a 2D array.
- Negative Indexing: You can use negative indices to access elements from the end of the array. For instance, arr[-1] accesses the last element in a 1D array, or arr[-1, -2] accesses the second-to-last element in the last row of a 2D array.

***Example:***

```
import numpy as np
arr = np.array([[1, 2, 3], [4, 5, 6], [7, 8, 9]])
print(arr[1, 2])    # Output: 6 (2nd row, 3rd column)
print(arr[-1, -1])  # Output: 9 (last row, last column)
```

### 2. Slicing in NumPy Arrays

Slicing lets you access a range of elements or a sub-array by specifying a start:stop:step format. Slicing is especially useful in larger arrays to extract parts without copying the data, which improves performance.

- 1D Array Slicing: A single : operator allows you to select a portion of a 1D array. For example, arr[1:4] selects elements from index 1 up to (but not including) index 4.
- 2D Array Slicing: You can slice along each dimension separately. For example, arr[0:2, 1:3] slices rows 0 to 1 and columns 1 to 2.
- Omitting Indices: If the start or stop values are omitted, they default to the beginning or end of the array, respectively. For example, arr[:3] retrieves elements from the beginning up to index 3.

**Example:**

```
arr = np.array([[1, 2, 3, 4], [5, 6, 7, 8], [9, 10, 11,
12]])
print(arr[1:, 1:3])  # Output: [[6 7] [10 11]] (slice of
rows 1 to end, columns 1 to 2)
```

### 3. Advanced Slicing and Indexing

- Step in Slicing: The step parameter allows you to skip elements. For example, arr[::2] returns every second element.
- Boolean Indexing: You can use boolean conditions to index arrays. For example, arr[arr > 5] returns all elements greater than 5.
- Fancy Indexing: You can use lists or arrays of indices to access multiple non-contiguous elements. For example, arr[[0, 2], [1, 3]] selects elements at positions (0,1) and (2,3).

***Example:***

```
arr = np.array([10, 20, 30, 40, 50])
print(arr[ ::2])            # Output: [10 30 50]
print(arr[arr > 25])        # Output: [30 40 50]
```

Using indexing and slicing effectively allows for efficient and concise code when working with arrays in data analysis and scientific computing, making NumPy highly powerful for such tasks.

## Attributes of an Array

Attributes of an array in NumPy provide information about the array's structure, contents, and memory layout.

***Here's a detailed look at these attributes:***

### 1. ndim (Number of Dimensions)

The ndim attribute represents the number of dimensions (axes) in an array. For example, a 1D array has ndim=1, a 2D array has ndim=2, and so on.It helps in determining whether the array is a vector, matrix, or higher-dimensional tensor.

***Example:***

```
import numpy as np
arr = np.array([[1, 2, 3], [4, 5, 6]])
print(arr.ndim)  # Output: 2 (since it's a 2D array)
```

### 2. shape (Dimensions of the Array)

The shape attribute is a tuple that gives the size of each dimension in an array. For example, a 3x4 matrix will have a shape of (3, 4).It's especially useful for reshaping and verifying the structure of arrays for compatibility in operations.

***Example:***

```
arr = np.array([[1, 2, 3], [4, 5, 6]])
print(arr.shape)  # Output: (2, 3) indicating 2 rows and 3
columns
```

### 3. size (Total Number of Elements)

The size attribute provides the total number of elements in the array, which is the product of all dimensions.It helps in understanding the memory usage and the scale of data stored in the array.

***Example:***

```
arr = np.array([[1, 2, 3], [4, 5, 6]])
print(arr.size)  # Output: 6 (2 rows * 3 columns)
```

### 4. dtype (Data Type of Elements)

The dtype attribute represents the data type of elements stored in the array, such as int32, float64, bool, etc.Knowing dtype is crucial for type-specific operations and to ensure accuracy in calculations.

***Example:***

```
arr = np.array([1, 2, 3], dtype=np.float32)
print(arr.dtype)  # Output: float32
```

### 5. itemsize (Bytes Per Element)

The itemsize attribute shows the memory size in bytes for each element in the array.This attribute, combined with size, gives a good understanding of the array's memory consumption (size * itemsize).

***Example:***

```
arr = np.array([1, 2, 3], dtype=np.int32)
print(arr.itemsize)  # Output: 4 (since int32 requires 4
bytes)
```

These attributes allow for efficient data manipulation and insight into the structure and requirements of arrays in data analysis and scientific computing. Important attributes of a NumPy array for a quick and clear understanding (Table 6.2).

**Table 6.2: Attributes of a NumPy Array**

| Attribute | Description | Example Code | Example Output |
|---|---|---|---|
| **ndim** | Number of dimensions (axes) of the array | arr.ndim | 2 for a 2D array |
| **shape** | Dimensions of the array as a tuple | arr.shape | (3, 4) for 3x4 array |
| **size** | Total number of elements in the array | arr.size | 12 for 3x4 array |
| **dtype** | Data type of elements in the array | arr.dtype | float32 |
| **itemsize** | Memory size of each element in bytes | a r r . itemsize | 4 bytes for int32 elements |

## Pandas

Pandas is a popular Python library widely used for data manipulation and analysis, especially in fields like data science, finance, and machine learning. Built on top of NumPy, Pandas provides high-level data structures, like Series and DataFrame, which simplify handling and transforming large datasets. The Series is a one-dimensional labeled array capable of holding data of any type, similar to a list or a NumPy array but with custom labels (indices). The DataFrame, a two-dimensional labeled data structure, is more like an in-memory database table with rows and columns, allowing for easy manipulation, selection, and data alignment. Pandas' flexibility in handling data from various sources (e.g., CSV, Excel, SQL databases) is one of its standout features, making it essential for tasks involving structured data.

One of the strengths of Pandas lies in its extensive functionality for data manipulation and cleaning. For instance, with Pandas, you can easily filter data, handle missing values, and reshape data formats. These operations are accomplished through powerful functions and intuitive syntax. Operations like df.fillna() to handle missing data, df.drop() to remove rows or columns, and df.groupby() for aggregating data by specific categories are essential for data cleaning. Additionally, Pandas supports complex operations like merging, joining, and concatenating data across multiple DataFrames, which is crucial when working with real-world, multi-source data. The .apply() and .map() functions allow custom transformations to be applied to data, making it extremely flexible for tailored data processing.Pandas also provides robust tools for data analysis and visualization. Descriptive statistics can be easily generated using methods like .describe() and .value_counts(), offering quick insights into data distribution and frequency. Additionally, Pandas integrates seamlessly with visualization libraries like Matplotlib and Seaborn, allowing users to plot histograms, scatter plots, and line graphs directly from DataFrames. This direct integration enables users to explore and visualize data in a highly interactive and efficient manner, fostering faster and more informed decision-making in data projects. Overall, Pandas is invaluable for anyone dealing with data as it simplifies and streamlines the workflow from data import to analysis and visualization, making it an indispensable tool in the Python ecosystem.

## Series & Dataframe

In Pandas, both Series and DataFrame are foundational data structures for handling and manipulating data. They are designed to handle a wide variety of data types, perform complex operations, and make data manipulation intuitive and efficient.

- Here's a detailed explanation of both:

### Series

A Series is a one-dimensional labeled array that can hold any data type (integers, floats, strings, or Python objects). It's akin to a column in a table or a single row in a dataset and combines the flexibility of lists with the functionality of dictionaries due to its label-based indexing.

**Creating a Series:** Series can be created from lists, dictionaries, or scalar values.

```
import pandas as pd
# From a list
s1 = pd.Series([1, 2, 3, 4])
# From a dictionary
s2 = pd.Series({'a': 1, 'b': 2, 'c': 3})
# From a scalar with specified index
s3 = pd.Series(5, index=['x', 'y', 'z'])
```

**Accessing Data in a Series:** You can access elements in a Series either by position (using integer-based indexing) or by label (using dictionary-like key-based indexing).

```
print(s1[0])  # First element
print(s2['b'])  # Element with index 'b'
```

Operations on Series: A Series supports element-wise operations, including arithmetic, filtering, and aggregation functions. You can also apply functions to each element using .apply().

```
s4 = pd.Series([10, 20, 30])
print(s4 + 5)  # Adds 5 to each element
```

**Attributes of a Series:** Key attributes include s.index (for accessing the index), s.values (the array of values), and s.dtype (data type of the values).Series are ideal for working with one-dimensional data, making it easy to perform statistical and analytical tasks on isolated data columns or vectors.

## DataFrame

A DataFrame is a two-dimensional, labeled data structure that resembles a spreadsheet or SQL table. It consists of rows and columns and can hold multiple Series objects, each representing a column. DataFrames are highly flexible and are used to store and manipulate structured data.

### Creating a Data Frame

Data Frames can be created from various sources, including dictionaries of lists, lists of dictionaries, NumPy arrays, and even from existing Series:

From a dictionary of lists:

```
data = {
    'Name': ['Alice', 'Bob', 'Charlie'],
    'Age': [24, 30, 22],
    'City': ['New York', 'Los Angeles', 'Chicago']
}
df = pd.DataFrame(data)
```

From a list of dictionaries:

```
data = [
    {'Name': 'Alice', 'Age': 24},
    {'Name': 'Bob', 'Age': 30},
    {'Name': 'Charlie', 'Age': 22}
]
df = pd.DataFrame(data)
```

From Series:

```
names = pd.Series(['Alice', 'Bob', 'Charlie'])
ages = pd.Series([24, 30, 22])
df = pd.DataFrame({'Name': names, 'Age': ages})
```

### Accessing Data in a DataFrame

Data in a DataFrame can be accessed by both row and column:

### Accessing columns:

```
print(df['Name'])  # Access 'Name' column as a Series
```

**Accessing rows:**

Using loc for label-based indexing:

```
print(df.loc[0])  # First row
```

Using iloc for integer-based indexing:

```
print(df.iloc[1])  # Second row
```

### Operations on DataFrames

DataFrames support a wide range of operations, such as arithmetic, filtering, grouping, and data transformations:

**Arithmetic Operations:** You can perform arithmetic on individual columns or across multiple columns.

```
df['New_Column'] = df['Age'] * 2  # Adds a new column by multiplying 'Age' by 2
```

### Filtering and Masking:

```
adults = df[df['Age'] > 25]  # Filters rows where 'Age' is greater than 25
```

### Aggregation and Grouping:

```
avg_age = df['Age'].mean()  # Calculates the mean age
grouped = df.groupby('City')['Age'].mean()  # Group by 'City' and calculate mean age
```

Merging and Joining: DataFrames can be merged using merge() or concatenated with concat() to combine data from different sources.

- Important Attributes of DataFrames

### DataFrames come with several attributes:

- df.shape: Returns the (rows, columns) shape of the DataFrame.
- df.columns: Lists the column labels.
- df.dtypes: Shows the data type of each column.
- df.values: Provides the underlying data as a NumPy array.

### When to Use Series vs DataFrame

Use Series when you need to handle a single, one-dimensional column of data or perform operations on a single vector.Use DataFrame when working with multiple columns or a full dataset with various dimensions, as it offers more flexibility for complex data analysis and manipulation.Both Series and DataFrames are essential data structures in Pandas, catering to different aspects of data handling. Series is ideal for single-dimensional data, while DataFrames are versatile for handling multi-dimensional data structures with multiple rows and columns.

Together, they provide powerful tools for data manipulation, making Pandas an invaluable library for data analysis and scientific research.

## Operations on Dataframe

Operations on a DataFrame in Pandas are essential tools that enable you to manipulate and analyze structured data effectively. A DataFrame is a two-dimensional labeled data structure with columns of potentially different types. You can perform a wide variety of operations to filter, transform, and aggregate data, making Pandas an invaluable library for data science and data analysis. Below are some of the most common and important operations you can perform on a DataFrame.

### 1. Selection of Data (Rows and Columns)

One of the most fundamental operations is selecting data, whether it's specific columns or rows within the DataFrame.

Selecting Columns: You can select one or more columns from a DataFrame by referencing their column names. This can be done using the column names in square brackets.

```
df['column_name']  # Select a single column
df[['column1', 'column2']]  # Select multiple columns
```

**Selecting Rows:** Rows can be selected using integer-based indexing with iloc or label-based indexing with loc.

```
df.loc[0]  # Select the first row by label
df.iloc[0]  # Select the first row by index position
```

### 2. Filtering and Conditional Selection

You can filter the rows of a DataFrame based on conditions, which is a powerful tool for data analysis.

```
filtered_df = df[df['column_name'] > 10]  # Select rows
where the column value is greater than 10
filtered_df = df[(df['column1'] > 10) & (df['column2'] <
20)]  # Multiple conditions
```

This operation allows you to create a subset of the DataFrame where certain conditions are met, making it easier to focus on the data that matters.

### 3. Adding and Modifying Columns

Pandas allows you to add new columns or modify existing ones. This can be done by performing operations on other columns or constants.

**Adding a Column:** You can create a new column based on existing columns.

```
df['new_column'] = df['column1'] * 2  # Create a new column based on column1
```

**Modifying a Column:** You can modify an existing column by performing arithmetic or other operations on its values.

```
df['column_name'] = df['column_name'] + 5  # Modify values in a column
```

### 4. Dropping Rows and Columns

You can remove rows or columns from a DataFrame using the drop() method. This is useful for cleaning data by removing irrelevant or unnecessary information.

**Dropping Columns:** Use axis=1 to indicate that you are dropping a column.

```
df = df.drop('column_name', axis=1)  # Drop a column
```

**Dropping Rows:** Rows can be dropped by specifying their index.

```
df = df.drop(index)  # Drop rows by index
```

### 5. Arithmetic Operations

Pandas allows you to perform arithmetic operations on entire columns or between different columns, making it a powerful tool for calculating new metrics.

```
df['total'] = df['column1'] + df['column2']  # Add values in two columns
df['discounted_price'] = df['price'] * 0.9  # Apply a discount
```

You can also perform mathematical operations like addition, subtraction, multiplication, and division across the DataFrame.

### 6. Aggregation Functions

Aggregation functions allow you to summarize data by calculating metrics like sum, mean, median, count, etc. These operations are crucial for analyzing large datasets.

## Sum of a column:

```
total = df['column_name'].sum()
```

## Mean of a column:

```
mean_value = df['column_name'].mean()
```

## Count of non-null entries:

```
count = df['column_name'].count()
```

These functions are helpful for summarizing data and understanding trends within the dataset.

### 7. GroupBy Operations

The groupby() method is one of the most powerful features in Pandas. It allows you to group data based on specific columns and perform aggregation operations on each group.

```
grouped = df.groupby('group_column')['value_column'].sum()
# Sum values by group
```

You can also apply multiple aggregations to a grouped DataFrame:

```
grouped = df.groupby('group_column').agg({'value_column':
['sum', 'mean']})
```

This allows you to perform complex analyses, like comparing performance across different categories or groups within the data.

### 8. Sorting

Sorting data is important when you need to order it based on certain criteria. Pandas provides the sort_values() method to sort the data by one or more columns.

```
df = df.sort_values('column_name')  # Sort by a single
column

df = df.sort_values(['col1', 'col2'], ascending=[True,
False]) # Sort by multiple columns
```

### 9. Handling Missing Data

In real-world datasets, missing data is common. Pandas provides various methods for dealing with missing values, such as filling or dropping NaN (Not a Number) entries.

**Filling Missing Values:** Use fillna() to replace NaN values with a constant or the result of a method like forward filling or backward filling.

```
df = df.fillna(0)  # Replace NaN with 0
df = df.fillna(method='ffill')  # Forward fill NaN values
```

**Dropping Missing Values:** Use dropna() to remove rows containing NaN values.

```
df = df.dropna()  # Drop rows with NaN values
```

### 10. Merging and Joining

DataFrames can be merged or joined based on a common column, which is useful for combining data from different sources.

```
merged_df = pd.merge(df1, df2, on='key_column', how='inner')
# Inner join
concatenated_df = pd.concat([df1, df2], axis=0) #
Concatenate along rows
```

Operations on DataFrames are integral to data analysis, offering flexibility and efficiency when working with structured data. With operations like filtering, modifying, aggregating, and merging data, Pandas provides a robust toolkit for cleaning, transforming, and analyzing datasets. These operations allow you to derive insights and make informed decisions based on your data.

## Combining datasets

Combining datasets, merging, joining, and performing aggregation and grouping are essential operations in data manipulation and analysis using Pandas. These techniques allow you to combine multiple datasets, summarize information, and derive meaningful insights. Here's a detailed explanation of each operation:

### 1. Combining Datasets

Combining datasets involves combining two or more separate datasets into a single dataset, which may include concatenating rows or columns, or merging datasets based on common keys. The common operations for combining datasets include:

Concatenation (concat): This operation combines datasets along rows or columns. You can use pd.concat() to stack DataFrames vertically (along rows) or horizontally (along columns). It's particularly useful when you have datasets that share the same structure.

***Example:***

```
df_combined = pd.concat([df1, df2], axis=0)    # Stacks DataFrames vertically (rows)
df_combined = pd.concat([df1, df2], axis=1)    # Stacks DataFrames horizontally (columns)
```

In this example, axis=0 means stacking along rows, while axis=1 refers to stacking along columns.

**Append:** This method adds the rows of one DataFrame to another. It is similar to concat but specifically designed for adding rows.

***Example:***

```
df_combined = df1.append(df2)
```

By default, the append() method stacks rows from df2 onto df1. It can also be used with additional options to modify how the indices and columns are handled.

## 2. Merge and Join

Merging and joining are operations used to combine datasets based on common columns or indices. These are similar to SQL operations like JOIN.

**Merge (merge):** The merge() function combines two DataFrames based on one or more common columns. It works similarly to SQL's JOIN operation and allows you to specify different types of joins: inner, outer, left, and right.

***Example:***

```
merged_df = pd.merge(df1, df2, on='key_column', how='inner')
# Inner join on 'key_column'
```

In this example, on='key_column' specifies the column on which to merge, and how='inner' determines the type of join. The join types are:

- inner: Returns only the rows with matching values in both DataFrames.
- outer: Returns all rows from both DataFrames, with NaN where there are no matches.
- left: Returns all rows from the left DataFrame, and matching rows from the right.

- right: Returns all rows from the right DataFrame, and matching rows from the left.

**Join (join):** The join() method is a simpler way to combine two DataFrames based on their indices or a key column. This method is often used when the joining key is the index of the DataFrame.

***Example:***

```
df_joined = df1.join(df2, on='key_column', how='left')
```

Here, df1 is joined with df2 on the specified key_column, with a left join.

### 3. Aggregation and Grouping

Aggregation and grouping operations are fundamental for summarizing data. Grouping data into categories and applying aggregation functions helps in deriving insights from datasets.

**Group By:** The groupby() function is used to group data based on a particular column or multiple columns, and then you can apply aggregation functions like sum, mean, count, etc., to each group.

***Example:***

```
grouped    =    df.groupby('category_column').agg({'value_
column': 'sum'})
```

This groups the data by the category_column and then calculates the sum of the value_column for each category.

**Multiple Aggregations:** You can apply multiple aggregation functions to the grouped data. This is useful when you want to summarize data in more than one way.

***Example:***

```
grouped    =    df.groupby('category_column').agg({'value_
column': ['sum', 'mean', 'count']})
```

In this example, the sum, mean, and count of the value_column are computed for each group.

**Applying Custom Aggregation:** You can also define your own aggregation functions and apply them using apply().

***Example:***

```
def custom_agg(x):
    return x.max() - x.min()
grouped    =    df.groupby('category_column').agg({'value_
column': custom_agg})
```

This computes the range (maximum value minus minimum value) of the value_column for each category in category_column.

**Aggregating Multiple Columns:** You can also aggregate multiple columns at once.

***Example:***

```
grouped = df.groupby('category_column').agg({
    'value_column1': 'sum',
    'value_column2': 'mean'
})
```

Here, value_column1 is summed, and value_column2 is averaged for each group.

The ability to combine datasets, perform merges, and group data for aggregation is a critical component of data analysis. The merging and joining operations allow you to merge data based on common columns, while grouping and aggregation enable you to summarize data efficiently. These techniques are invaluable when working with complex data, helping to simplify and consolidate information for further analysis or reporting. Whether you are combining datasets, aggregating data, or creating summary statistics, Pandas offers powerful tools for each task.

## Summary

NumPy and Pandas are two essential Python libraries for numerical and data manipulation tasks. NumPy provides support for large, multi-dimensional arrays and matrices, along with mathematical functions that make it easy to perform element-wise operations, matrix operations, and access array attributes like shape, size, and dtype. It is widely used for scientific computing and efficient array manipulations. Pandas, on the other hand, offers two main data structures: Series (1D) and DataFrame (2D), making it ideal for handling structured data. With Pandas, users can perform data cleaning, transformation, merging, and aggregation, and use powerful functions like groupby() for summarization. Together, NumPy and Pandas make data analysis and mathematical operations efficient and scalable in Python.

## Exercise Questions

- Create a NumPy array with the elements 1 to 10 and perform element-wise addition of 5 to the array.
- Create a 2x3 NumPy array and find its shape and size.
- Perform matrix multiplication on two NumPy arrays using the np.dot() function.
- Write a Python program to slice a NumPy array and extract the first 3 elements.
- Create a NumPy array and access the element at index (2, 3) in a 2D array.
- Create a Pandas Series from a list of numbers and print it.
- Convert a Pandas Series to a DataFrame and perform basic operations (e.g., adding a new column).
- Load a dataset into a Pandas DataFrame and check the data types of its columns.
- Merge two DataFrames using a common column and print the result.
- Demonstrate the use of the groupby() function in Pandas to find the sum of a specific column for each group.
- Write a program to filter a DataFrame based on a condition (e.g., values greater than 50 in a specific column).
- Create a DataFrame and apply an aggregation function (e.g., mean()) to each column.
- Use indexing in NumPy to extract a subarray from the 2nd row of a 4x4 array.
- Write a Pandas program to join two DataFrames based on their index and display the result.
- Create a NumPy array with random values and find the maximum and minimum values in the array.

CHAPTER - 7

# Data Visualization & Seaborn

Data visualization is essential in transforming raw data into meaningful insights that can be easily interpreted. The necessity of data visualization lies in its ability to help individuals and organizations quickly understand and make sense of complex data, supporting decision-making, trend identification, and data-driven storytelling.

*Here are some of the key reasons why data visualization is critical (Figure 7.1):*

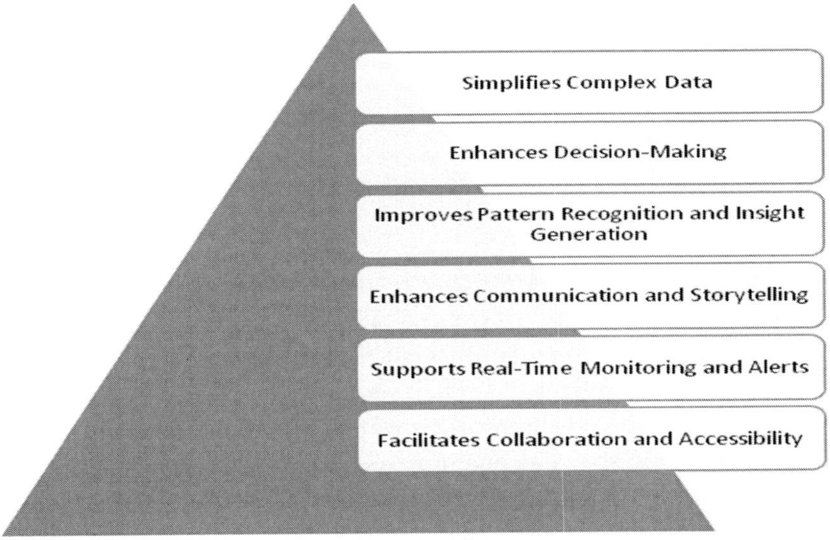


**Figure 7.1: Reasons for critical data visualization**

## 1. Simplifies Complex Data

In today's data-driven world, vast amounts of data are generated every second. Interpreting this raw data in numerical or textual form can be overwhelming, especially when dealing with large datasets. Visualization techniques such as charts, graphs, and maps distill complex data, making it easier to comprehend and interpret patterns, relationships, and anomalies. This helps individuals, including those without a technical background, to process complex information at a glance.

## 2. Enhances Decision-Making

Data visualization plays a crucial role in decision-making by allowing stakeholders to see trends and patterns that might go unnoticed in raw data. By highlighting correlations and trends, visualizations help decision-makers forecast outcomes, assess risks, and make informed choices based on data-driven insights. For example, a line graph showing an upward trend in sales over months can help a business predict future growth and allocate resources effectively.

## 3. Improves Pattern Recognition and Insight Generation

Humans are highly visual, with a significant part of the brain dedicated to processing visual information. Data visualization takes advantage of this ability, enabling people to spot trends, patterns, and outliers more quickly than they could by analyzing numbers alone. Bar charts, scatter plots, and heat maps help to identify relationships in the data and uncover insights that may lead to new hypotheses, further analysis, or actions.

## 4. Enhances Communication and Storytelling

Data visualization is a powerful communication tool that conveys insights effectively to diverse audiences. It bridges the gap between data scientists and business professionals by translating quantitative findings into visual stories that are intuitive and accessible. Visual storytelling makes presentations more engaging and helps people retain information longer. For instance, a well-designed dashboard can present a story about business performance by combining various data points into one cohesive narrative.

## 5. Supports Real-Time Monitoring and Alerts

For industries where timely decision-making is essential, such as healthcare, finance, and retail, real-time data visualization enables quick monitoring and response. Dashboards displaying key performance indicators (KPIs) allow users to track metrics in real time and respond to anomalies or potential issues immediately. For instance, in e-commerce, visual dashboards monitoring website traffic or transaction volumes can alert operators to potential problems like system slowdowns, allowing for rapid intervention.

## 6. Facilitates Collaboration and Accessibility

Visualized data is easier to share and discuss within teams, enhancing collaborative decision-making. By presenting data in a visual format, everyone—regardless of technical expertise—can contribute to discussions, offering diverse perspectives and insights. Tools like dashboards, interactive charts, and shared visual reports facilitate collaborative analysis, enabling various team members to draw conclusions together, making visualization an accessible bridge for all departments.

## Matplotlib

Matplotlib is a powerful and flexible Python library that enables the creation of a wide range of static, animated, and interactive visualizations. It is particularly well-known for its ability to produce publication-quality plots and its versatility in handling different types of data. With Matplotlib, users can generate simple plots like line and scatter plots, or more complex visualizations like histograms, heatmaps, and 3D plots. Its intuitive interface and integration with other data analysis libraries, such as NumPy and pandas, make it a popular choice for data scientists and analysts for visualizing data patterns, distributions, and trends.The library offers fine-grained control over the appearance of the plots, including customizations for axes, labels, titles, and legends. It supports multiple plotting styles and themes, which can be applied to enhance the visual appeal or meet specific publication standards. Additionally, Matplotlib's flexibility allows users to create subplots, customize grid lines, and annotate charts to improve the interpretability of data. Whether for quick exploratory analysis or creating complex visual representations for presentations, Matplotlib serves as an essential tool in the data visualization toolkit, aiding in effective communication of insights drawn from data.

- Here's an overview of some common plot types you can create with Matplotlib:

### 1. Line Plot

Line plots are ideal for visualizing trends over time or showing the relationship between two continuous variables, as they highlight how one variable changes in relation to another. By plotting data points along the x and y axes and connecting them with straight lines, line plots provide a clear view of patterns, fluctuations, and overall trends in the data. In Matplotlib, you can create a line plot using the plot() function, where the x-values typically represent time or an independent variable, and the y-values represent the dependent variable. This type of plot is especially useful in time series analysis, financial data visualization, and other fields where understanding the progression or trend of data is crucial.

***Example:*** A line plot is ideal for visualizing monthly sales figures or tracking stock prices over time.

```
import matplotlib.pyplot as plt
plt.plot([1, 2, 3, 4], [10, 20, 25, 30])
plt.title("Simple Line Plot")
plt.xlabel("X-axis")
plt.ylabel("Y-axis")
plt.show()
```

## 2. Bar Chart

Bar charts are an effective way to compare categorical data, as they visually display the quantities or counts for different categories. Each bar represents a category, with its height corresponding to the value of the data for that category. Bar charts make it easy to see comparisons between distinct groups, helping to highlight trends, differences, or distributions in the data. In Matplotlib, you can create a bar chart using the bar() function, where the x-axis represents the categories, and the y-axis shows the values associated with each category. Bar charts are widely used in various fields, such as marketing to compare product sales, education to compare exam scores, and economics to compare financial indicators across sectors.

***Example:*** A bar chart could be used to show the sales revenue for different products in a store.

```
categories = ['Product A', 'Product B', 'Product C']
values = [100, 150, 200]
plt.bar(categories, values)
plt.title("Sales by Product")
plt.xlabel("Products")
plt.ylabel("Sales")
plt.show()
```

## 3. Histogram

Histograms are useful for visualizing the distribution of a single continuous variable, as they show how data is spread across different ranges. They help in understanding the frequency or count of data points within specific intervals or bins. In a histogram, the x-axis represents the range of values (divided into bins), and the y-axis shows the frequency of data points that fall into each bin. The hist() function in Matplotlib is used to create histograms, where it automatically divides the data into bins and displays the number of data points that fall into each bin. This type of plot is commonly used in statistics and data analysis to observe the shape of a dataset's distribution, such as normal, skewed, or bimodal distributions.

***Example:*** A histogram can be used to analyze the distribution of test scores among students.

```
import numpy as np
data = np.random.normal(50, 10, 100)
plt.hist(data, bins=10)
plt.title("Histogram of Test Scores")
plt.xlabel("Scores")
plt.ylabel("Frequency")
plt.show()
```

## 4. Scatter Plot

Scatter plots are ideal for displaying the relationship or correlation between two numerical variables, as they show how one variable changes in relation to another. Each point on the scatter plot represents a pair of values, one from each variable, plotted along the x and y axes. Scatter plots are particularly useful for identifying patterns, clusters, or outliers in the data. In Matplotlib, the scatter() function is used to create scatter plots, where individual points are plotted without connecting them with lines. This type of plot is often used in regression analysis, to visualize correlations, or to detect trends in data, such as positive, negative, or no correlation between the variables.

***Example:*** A scatter plot can visualize the relationship between age and income.

```
x = [10, 20, 30, 40]
y = [15, 25, 35, 45]
plt.scatter(x, y)
plt.title("Age vs. Income Scatter Plot")
plt.xlabel("Age")
plt.ylabel("Income")
plt.show()
```

## 5. Boxplot

Boxplots are used to show the distribution of a dataset through five key summary statistics: minimum, first quartile, median, third quartile, and maximum. This plot highlights outliers and variability in data. The boxplot() function in Matplotlib creates boxplots, often for comparing distributions across different categories.

***Example:*** Boxplots are commonly used to show the spread of test scores across multiple classes.

```
data = [np.random.normal(50, 10, 100), np.random.normal(60,
15, 100)]
plt.boxplot(data)
plt.title("Boxplot of Two Classes")
plt.xlabel("Class")
plt.ylabel("Scores")
plt.show()
```

## Seaborn

Seaborn is a powerful and easy-to-use data visualization library built on top of Matplotlib in Python. It is specifically designed to make complex statistical plots simpler and more attractive, with a focus on data visualization for statistical analysis. Seaborn integrates seamlessly with pandas DataFrames, allowing users to plot directly from data structures like pandas Series and DataFrames. It provides a high-level interface for drawing a variety of attractive and informative statistical graphics, such as box plots, violin plots, pair plots, heatmaps, and more. Seaborn also improves the aesthetics of visualizations by providing better color schemes, styling options, and default themes, making it easier to create polished, publication-ready charts with minimal code.What sets Seaborn apart from other visualization libraries is its ability to create complex plots with simple commands. It includes functions for visualizing relationships between variables, distribution of data, and comparing multiple categories with ease. Seaborn's visualization capabilities are particularly useful for exploratory data analysis (EDA), as it helps reveal patterns, trends, and correlations in large datasets. Additionally, Seaborn works well with other scientific libraries like NumPy and SciPy, enabling users to perform in-depth statistical analysis while creating visually appealing plots. Its integration with Matplotlib allows for further customization and refinement of visualizations when needed.

Seaborn provides a wide range of useful plots for exploring and visualizing data, each serving a specific purpose in data analysis. Below is a brief explanation of the most common plot types you can create using Seaborn:

**Box Plot:** A box plot is a powerful way to visualize the distribution of data, especially to identify outliers. It displays the median, quartiles, and potential outliers in a dataset. The box represents the interquartile range (IQR) between the 25th and 75th percentiles, while the line inside the box shows the median. Whiskers extend from the box to the maximum and minimum data points within a certain range, and points outside this range are considered outliers. Box plots are useful for comparing the distribution of a variable across different categories.

## Usage in Seaborn: sns.boxplot()

**Bar Chart:** Bar charts are used to compare quantities across different categories. Each bar represents a category, with the height of the bar corresponding to the value or count of data in that category. Bar charts can be vertical or horizontal, and Seaborn makes it easy to plot them with categorical data. They are especially useful for summarizing data distributions or comparing group sizes.

## Usage in Seaborn: sns.barplot(), sns.countplot()

**Scatter Plot:** Scatter plots display the relationship between two continuous variables. Each point on the plot represents one observation, with its position determined by the values of the two variables. Scatter plots are useful for identifying patterns, correlations, or clusters in the data. In Seaborn, scatter plots are particularly effective for visualizing linear or non-linear relationships.

## Usage in Seaborn: sns.scatterplot()

**Pair Plot:** Pair plots are an excellent way to visualize the relationships between multiple variables in a dataset. This plot creates a matrix of scatter plots for each pair of variables, as well as histograms or KDE (Kernel Density Estimation) plots along the diagonal. Pair plots are particularly helpful in identifying correlations and distributions of different features within the dataset.

## Usage in Seaborn: sns.pairplot()

**Heatmap:** Heatmaps are used to visualize matrix-like data, where values are represented by varying colors in a grid. They are particularly useful for visualizing correlations between numerical variables or any matrix data. In a heatmap, each cell represents the value at the intersection of two variables, and the color intensity reflects the magnitude of the value. Heatmaps are commonly used for visualizing correlation matrices and results from machine learning algorithms.

## Usage in Seaborn: sns.heatmap()

**Distribution Plot:** Distribution plots help visualize the distribution of a single variable. Seaborn offers several ways to visualize distributions, including histograms, KDEs (Kernel Density Estimation), and ECDFs (Empirical Cumulative Distribution Functions). These plots help understand the underlying distribution of data, detect skewness, identify peaks, and spot outliers. A distribution plot is particularly helpful for checking normality and other statistical properties of the data.

## Usage in Seaborn: sns.displot(), sns.kdeplot()

Each of these visualizations in Seaborn offers a high-level interface for creating informative and visually appealing charts, making it easier to explore relationships within data and draw meaningful insights.

## Summary

Data visualization is a crucial tool for understanding complex data by presenting it in graphical formats, allowing patterns, trends, and insights to be easily identified. Matplotlib is a powerful Python library for creating various types of plots like line plots, bar charts, histograms, scatter plots, and box plots, which are essential for visualizing numerical data and relationships. Seaborn, built on top of Matplotlib, offers enhanced functionality and aesthetics for creating more complex visualizations, such as pair plots, heatmaps, and distribution plots. These libraries help transform raw data into visual representations, enabling better decision-making, communication of findings, and easier interpretation of datasets.

## Exercise Questions

- Create a line plot of a dataset showing the relationship between two variables in Matplotlib.
- Plot a bar chart comparing the sales of five different products using Matplotlib.
- Generate a histogram using Matplotlib to display the distribution of a dataset of ages.
- Create a scatter plot to visualize the correlation between two numerical variables in a dataset.
- Generate a boxplot using Matplotlib to show the distribution of exam scores.
- Use Seaborn to create a box plot showing the distribution of a continuous variable across different categories.
- Plot a bar chart using Seaborn to compare average heights across different age groups.
- Create a scatter plot using Seaborn to visualize the relationship between two variables.
- Use Seaborn to generate a pair plot to visualize relationships between multiple variables in a dataset.
- Create a heatmap using Seaborn to visualize the correlation matrix of a dataset.
- Generate a distribution plot using Seaborn to visualize the distribution of a set of data points.
- Use Matplotlib to combine a line plot and scatter plot on the same graph.
- Create a boxplot in Seaborn to visualize the spread of data and identify outliers.

- Plot a line plot and a bar chart on the same figure using Matplotlib and compare them.
- Customize the appearance of a heatmap using Seaborn by changing color palettes and adding annotations.

## Books for Further Reading

- Automate the Boring Stuff with Python: Practical Programming for Total Beginners by Al Sweigart
- Fluent Python: Clear, Concise, and Effective Programming by Luciano Ramalho
- Python for Data Analysis: Data Wrangling with Pandas, NumPy, and IPython by Wes McKinney
- Python Programming: An Introduction to Computer Science by John Zelle
- Python Cookbook by David Beazley and Brian K. Jones
- Head First Python by Paul Barry
- The Pragmatic Programmer: Your Journey to Mastery by Andrew Hunt and David Thomas
- Effective Python: 90 Specific Ways to Write Better Python by Brett Slatkin

# References


[1] J. Guo, A. Ye, X. Wang, and Z. Guan, "OpenSeesPyView: Python programming-based visualization and post-processing tool for OpenSeesPy," *SoftwareX*, 2023, doi: 10.1016/j.softx.2022.101278.

[2] T. Georgieva-Trifonova, "Establishing Cross-Curricular Connections Through Python Programming in Computer Modeling Education," *TEM J.*, 2023, doi: 10.18421/TEM123-61.

[3] L. Sun and J. Liu, "Effects of Gamified Python Programming on Primary School Students' Computational Thinking Skills: A Differential Analysis of Gender," *J. Educ. Comput. Res.*, 2024, doi: 10.1177/07356331231225269.

[4] "PYTHON PROGRAMMING-APPLICATIONS AND FUTURE," *Int. J. Adv. Eng. Res. Dev.*, 2017, doi: 10.21090/ijaerd.it032.

[5] C. W. Okonkwo and A. Ade-Ibijola, "Python-bot: A chatbot for teaching python programming," *Eng. Lett.*, 2021.

[6] S. Banerjee, S. Seth, T. Dey, and D. Pal, "Python Programming Language and Its Scope in Future," *Int. Res. J. Mod. Eng. Technol. Sci.*, 2022.

[7] X. Cai, H. P. Langtangen, and H. Moe, "On the performance of the Python programming language for serial and parallel scientific computations," *Sci. Program.*, 2005, doi: 10.1155/2005/619804.

[8] T. C. Hsiao, Y. H. Chuang, C. Y. Chang, T. L. Chen, H. B. Zhang, and J. C. Chang, "Combining Building Block Process With Computational Thinking Improves Learning Outcomes of Python Programming With Peer Assessment," *SAGE Open*, 2023, doi: 10.1177/21582440231217715.

[9] "Python programming on win32," *Comput. Math. with Appl.*, 2000, doi: 10.1016/s0898-1221(00)90197-4.

[10] H. Bin Mehare, J. P. Anilkumar, and N. A. Usmani, "The Python Programming Language," in *A Guide to Applied Machine Learning for Biologists*, 2023. doi: 10.1007/978-3-031-22206-1_2.

[11] D. Lakshminarayanan and S. Prabhakaran, "A Study on Python Programming Language," *Dogo Rangsang Res. J. UGC Care Gr. I J.*, 2020.

[12] G. Van Rossum and U. Swallow, "Python ( programming language )," *Tutorials Point Pvt. Ltd.*, 2011.

[13] R. C. Tripathi, "Python: The future programming language," *Asian J. Multidimens. Res.*, 2021, doi: 10.5958/2278-4853.2021.01067.3.

[14] M. Schnieder and S. Williams, "Educational Mobile Apps for Programming in Python: Review and Analysis," *Educ. Sci.*, 2023, doi: 10.3390/educsci13010066.

[15] M. S. Prokopyev, E. Z. Vlasova, T. V. Tretyakova, M. A. Sorochinsky, and R. A. Solovyeva, "Development of a Programming Course for Students of a Teacher Training Higher Education Institution Using the Programming Language Python," *Propósitos y Represent.*, 2020, doi: 10.20511/pyr2020.v8n3.484.

[16] U. Bhimavarapu and J. D. Hemanth, "Python Basics," in *Learning Professional Python*, 2023. doi: 10.1201/9781003414322-1.

[17] T. Barua, R. Doshi, and K. K. Hiran, "2 Python basics," in *Mobile Applications Development*, 2020. doi: 10.1515/9783110689488-002.

[18] T. Weimin, Numpy, T. Weimin, and None, "Python for Data Science Cheat Sheet Python Basics," *2017-02-21*, 2018.

[19] Q. Kong, T. Siauw, and A. M. Bayen, "Python Basics," in *Python Programming and Numerical Methods*, 2021. doi: 10.1016/b978-0-12-819549-9.00010-5.

[20] D. Lafuente *et al.*, "A Gentle Introduction to Machine Learning for Chemists: An Undergraduate Workshop Using Python Notebooks for Visualization, Data Processing, Analysis, and Modeling," *J. Chem. Educ.*, 2021, doi: 10.1021/acs.jchemed.1c00142.

[21] B. Ballmann, "Python Basics," 2012. doi: 10.1007/978-3-642-24305-9_3.

[22] M. L. Hetland, *Python algorithms: Mastering basic algorithms in the python language*. 2014. doi: 10.1007/978-1-4842-0055-1.

[23] P. Gupta and A. Bagchi, "Python Language Basics," 2024. doi: 10.1007/978-3-031-43725-0_3.

[24] A. Sitio, A. Sindar, M. Marbun, D. Tiara, and A. Aswin, "Pengenalan Data Scientist Pada Peserta PKBM AL HABIB Melalui Belajar Dasar Coding Python," *J. Pengabdi. Pada Masy.*, 2022, doi: 10.30653/002.202271.44.

[25] J. M. Stewart and M. Mommert, "Basic Python," in *Python for Scientists*, 2023. doi: 10.1017/9781009029728.004.

[26] J. Melorose, R. Perroy, and S. Careas, "Python for data science: Python basics," *Statew. Agric. L. Use Baseline 2015*, 2015.

## Programming for Problem Solving-II [Python]

### (Prerequisite: Programming for Problem Solving-I [C] - Theory & Lab)

### (Lab based on the theory subject - Programming for Problem Solving-II [Python])

### List of Suggestive Experiments Programming for Problem Solving-II [Python]

### Lab

**CO1- Part A: To familiarize with Python programming (Any 3).**

1. **Write a Python program to accept three sides of a triangle as the input and print whether the triangle is valid or not.**

**Ans1: # Function to check if a triangle is valid**

```
def is_valid_triangle(a, b, c):
    # A triangle is valid if the sum of any two sides is greater than the third side
    return a + b > c and a + c > b and b + c > a
# Accept three sides as input
try:
    a = float(input("Enter the length of the first side of the triangle: "))
    b = float(input("Enter the length of the second side of the triangle: "))
    c = float(input("Enter the length of the third side of the triangle: "))
    # Check if the triangle is valid
    if is_valid_triangle(a, b, c):
        print("The triangle is valid.")
    else:
        print("The triangle is not valid.")
except ValueError:
    print("Please enter valid numerical values for the sides.")
```

2. **Write a Python program to find the largest among three numbers.**

**Ans2:** # Function to find the largest among three numbers

```
def find_largest(a, b, c):
    if a ⩾ b and a ⩾ c:
        return a
    elif b ⩾ a and b ⩾ c:
        return b
    else:
        return c
# Accept three numbers as input
try:
    a = float(input("Enter the first number: "))
    b = float(input("Enter the second number: "))
    c = float(input("Enter the third number: "))
        # Find and print the largest number
    largest = find_largest(a, b, c)
    print("The largest number is:", largest)
except ValueError:
    print("Please enter valid numerical values.")
```

3. **Write a program to check if the given number is a palindrome number.**

**Ans3:** # Function to check if a number is a palindrome

```
def is_palindrome(number):
    # Convert the number to a string
    num_str = str(number)
    # Check if the string is the same when reversed
    return num_str == num_str[::-1]

# Accept a number as input
try:
    number = int(input("Enter a number: "))

    # Check if the number is a palindrome
    if is_palindrome(number):
        print(f"The number {number} is a palindrome.")
```

```
    else:
        print(f"The number {number} is not a palindrome.")
except ValueError:
    print("Please enter a valid integer.")
```

4. **Write a Program to reverse a user entered number and determine whether the original and reversed numbers are equal or not.**

   **Ans 4: # Function to reverse a number**

```
def reverse_number(number):
    # Convert the number to a string, reverse it, and convert
it back to an integer
    reversed_num = int(str(number)[::-1])
    return reversed_num


# Accept a number as input
try:
    number = int(input("Enter a number: "))


    # Reverse the number
    reversed_num = reverse_number(number)


    # Check if the original and reversed numbers are equal
    if number == reversed_num:
        print(f"The original number {number} and the reversed
number {reversed_num} are equal. It is a palindrome.")
    else:
        print(f"The original number {number} and the reversed
number {reversed_num} are not equal.")
except ValueError:
    print("Please enter a valid integer.")
```

**CO1- Part B: Solve different string manipulation tasks (Any 2).**

5. **Write a program to count the number of alphabets and number of digits in a string.**

   **Ans5:** # Function to count alphabets and digits in a string

```
def count_alphabets_digits(input_string):
    alphabets = 0
    digits = 0
    for char in input_string:
        if char.isalpha():
            alphabets += 1
        elif char.isdigit():
            digits += 1
    return alphabets, digits

# Accept a string as input
input_string = input("Enter a string: ")

# Count alphabets and digits
alphabets, digits = count_alphabets_digits(input_string)

# Display the results
print(f"Number of alphabets: {alphabets}")
print(f"Number of digits: {digits}")
```

**6. Write a Python function that takes a string as input and returns a new string where the first letter of each word is capitalized.**

**Ans 6:** # Function to capitalize the first letter of each word in a string

```
def capitalize_words(input_string):
    return input_string.title()

# Accept a string as input
input_string = input("Enter a string: ")

# Capitalize the first letter of each word
capitalized_string = capitalize_words(input_string)

# Display the result
print("String with capitalized words:", capitalized_string)
```

7. **Write a program to accept a string from the user, delete all vowels from the string and display the result.**

**Ans7:** # Function to remove vowels from a string

```
def remove_vowels(input_string):
    vowels = "aeiouAEIOU"
    result = ''.join([char for char in input_string if char not in vowels])
    return result

# Accept a string as input
input_string = input("Enter a string: ")

# Remove vowels from the string
no_vowels_string = remove_vowels(input_string)

# Display the result
print("String after removing vowels:", no_vowels_string)
```

8. **Given a string, write a Python program to find the largest substring of uppercase characters and print the length of that substring.**

**Ans 8:** # Function to find the longest uppercase substring

```
def longest_uppercase_substring(input_string):
    max_length = 0
    current_length = 0

    for char in input_string:
        if char.isupper():
            current_length += 1
            max_length = max(max_length, current_length)
        else:
            current_length = 0  # Reset current length if a lowercase or non-alphabet character is found

    return max_length
```

```
# Accept a string as input
input_string = input("Enter a string: ")


# Find the length of the longest uppercase substring
max_uppercase_length = longest_uppercase_substring(input_
string)


# Display the result
print("Length of the longest uppercase substring:", max_
uppercase_length)
```

**CO2: Apply data structures such as lists, tuples, sets, and dictionaries (Any 4).**

**9. Suppose you want to know the total score of the Indian cricket team in a given match. To do so, your task is to find the sum of all the scores of the Indian team players. The scores are provided as a list, with each element as an individual score of the players. Also, there is a condition that if the number of elements in the list is more than 11, then it is an invalid input and the output should be -1.**

**Ans 9:** def total_score(scores):

```
# Check if the number of players is more than 11
if len(scores) > 11:
    return -1
# Calculate and return the total score
return sum(scores)


# Example with valid input
scores = [50, 30, 20, 40, 10, 60, 90, 30, 20, 50, 80]
print(total_score(scores))  # Output: 480


# Example with invalid input (more than 11 scores)
scores = [50, 30, 20, 40, 10, 60, 90, 30, 20, 50, 80, 100]
print(total_score(scores))  # Output: -1
```

**10. Write a program to create following 3 lists:**

- A list of names.
- A list of employee's ids.
- A list of salaries.

From these lists, generate 3 tuples - one containing all names, another containing all ids and third containing all salaries.

Also, from the three created lists, generate and print a list of tuples containing name, ids and salaries.

**Ans10:** # List of names

```
names = ["John", "Alice", "Bob", "Emma", "David"]

# List of employee IDs
employee_ids = [101, 102, 103, 104, 105]

# List of salaries
salaries = [50000, 60000, 45000, 55000, 70000]

# Displaying the lists
print("Names:", names)
print("Employee IDs:", employee_ids)
print("Salaries:", salaries)
```

**11. Write a program to create a set containing 10 randomly generated numbers in the range 15 to 45. Count how many of these numbers are less than 30. Delete all numbers which are greater than 35.**

**Ans11:** import random

```
# Create a set with 10 randomly generated numbers between 15
and 45
random_numbers = set(random.randint(15, 45) for _ in range(10))

# Count how many of these numbers are less than 30
count_less_than_30 = sum(1 for num in random_numbers if num
< 30)

# Delete all numbers greater than 35
random_numbers = {num for num in random_numbers if num ⩽ 35}
```

```
# Display the results
print("Random numbers:", random_numbers)
print("Count of numbers less than 30:", count_less_than_30)
```

**12. Write a Python program to check whether an element exists within a tuple.**

**13. Create a dictionary of 10 usernames and passwords. Receive the username and password from keyboard and search for them in the dictionary. Print appropriate message on the screen based on whether a match is found or not.**

**Ans 13:** # Creating a dictionary with 10 usernames and passwords

```
user_credentials = {
    "john_doe": "password123",
    "alice_smith": "alice2023",
    "bob_jones": "bob1234",
    "emma_williams": "emma5678",
    "david_clark": "david999",
    "susan_martin": "susan@2024",
    "paul_lee": "paul12345",
    "maria_garcia": "maria2024",
    "james_brown": "james@123",
    "linda_wilson": "linda4567"
}

# Receiving username and password from the user
username_input = input("Enter your username: ")
password_input = input("Enter your password: ")

# Checking if the username and password match
if username_input in user_credentials and user_credentials[username_input] == password_input:
    print("Login successful!")
else:
    print("Invalid username or password. Please try again.")
```

**14. You are provided with a dictionary containing the names of different football clubs as keys and the name of the main player of the corresponding team as values. When the main player of a team retires, one of their teammates steps up to fill in their role as the main player.**

**You're also provided with a list which contains the names of the football clubs for which the current main players are retiring and the names of the corresponding new main player. Your task is to update the values in the original dictionary with the names of the new main players.**

**Ans 14:** # Original dictionary containing football clubs and their main players

```
football_clubs = {
    "FC Barcelona": "Lionel Messi",
    "Real Madrid": "Cristiano Ronaldo",
    "Manchester United": "Bruno Fernandes",
    "Liverpool": "Mohamed Salah",
    "Bayern Munich": "Robert Lewandowski"
}

# List of retiring players and their corresponding new main players
retiring_players = [
    ("FC Barcelona", "Robert Lewandowski"),
    ("Real Madrid", "Vinicius Jr."),
    ("Liverpool", "Darwin Núñez")
]

# Updating the dictionary with new main players
for club, new_player in retiring_players:
    if club in football_clubs:
        football_clubs[club] = new_player

# Display the updated dictionary
print("Updated Football Clubs and Main Players:")
for club, player in football_clubs.items():
    print(f"{club}: {player}")
```

**CO3: Organize and utilize functions to modularize code and improve reusability (Any 2).**

**15. Write a program that defines a function compute ( ) that calculates the value of n + nn + nnn + nnnn, where n is digit received by the function. Test the function for digits 4 and 7.**

**Ans 15:** def compute(n):

```
    # Convert n to string and concatenate to form nn, nnn, nnnn
    n1 = int(str(n))
    n2 = int(str(n) * 2)
    n3 = int(str(n) * 3)
    n4 = int(str(n) * 4)

    # Calculate the result
    result = n1 + n2 + n3 + n4
    return result

# Test the function for digits 4 and 7
print("Result for n = 4:", compute(4))
print("Result for n = 7:", compute(7))
```

**16. Create a lambda function 'greater', which takes two arguments x and y and return x if x > y otherwise y.**

**Ans 16:** # Lambda function 'greater'

```
greater = lambda x, y: x if x > y else y

# Test the lambda function
print(greater(10, 5))  # Output: 10
print(greater(3, 8))   # Output: 8
```

**17. Write a Python program to demonstrate the use of lambda functions with map, filter, and reduce.**

**Ans 17:** from functools import reduce

```
# Sample list of numbers
numbers = [1, 2, 3, 4, 5, 6, 7, 8, 9]
```

```
# 1. Using lambda with map:
# Multiply each element by 2 using map and lambda
mapped_result = list(map(lambda x: x * 2, numbers))
print("Result of map (multiply by 2):", mapped_result)

# 2. Using lambda with filter:
# Filter out all numbers greater than 5 using filter and
lambda
filtered_result = list(filter(lambda x: x > 5, numbers))
print("Result of filter (numbers > 5):", filtered_result)

# 3. Using lambda with reduce:
# Find the sum of all numbers using reduce and lambda
sum_result = reduce(lambda x, y: x + y, numbers)
print("Result of reduce (sum of all numbers):", sum_result)
```

**CO4: Utilize Error handling techniques (Any 2).**

**18. Write a Python program to handle a Zero Division Error exception when dividing a number by zero.**

**Ans 18:** # Function to divide two numbers

```
def divide_numbers(num1, num2):
    try:
        # Attempt to divide num1 by num2
        result = num1 / num2
    except ZeroDivisionError:
        # Handle ZeroDivisionError
        return "Error: Cannot divide by zero!"
    else:
        # Return the result if no exception occurs
        return f"The result of division is: {result}"

# Test the function
print(divide_numbers(10, 2))  # Valid division
print(divide_numbers(10, 0))  # Division by zero
```

**19. Write a Python program that prompts the user to input an integer and raises a Value Error exception if the input is not a valid integer.**

**Ans19:** # Function to prompt user for an integer input

```
def get_integer_input():
    try:
        # Prompting user for input
        user_input = input("Please enter an integer: ")

        # Try to convert the input to an integer
        num = int(user_input)
        return num

    except ValueError:
        # If the input is not a valid integer, raise a ValueError
        print("Error: Invalid input! Please enter a valid integer.")
        raise ValueError("Input is not a valid integer.")

# Test the function
try:
    result = get_integer_input()
    print(f"You entered the integer: {result}")
except ValueError:
    print("Program terminated due to invalid input.")
```

**20. Implement an interactive calculator in which user input is assumed to be a formula that consist of a number, an operator (at least + and -), and another number, separated by white space (e.g. 1 + 1). Split user input using str.split(), and check whether the resulting list is valid:**

- If the input does not consist of 3 elements, raise a Formula Error, which is a custom Exception.
- Try to convert the first and third input to a float (like so: float_value = float(str_value)). Catch any Value

Error that occurs, and instead raise a Formula Error.

- If the second input is not '+' or '-', again raise a Formula Error.

If the input is valid, perform the calculation and print out the result. The user is then prompted to provide new input,and so on, until the user enters quit.

**Ans 20:** class FormulaError(Exception):

```
    """Custom exception for invalid formulas."""
    pass


def calculate():
    while True:
        user_input = input("Enter a formula (e.g., '1 + 1')
or 'quit' to exit: ").strip()

        # Exit condition
        if user_input.lower() == 'quit':
            print("Exiting the calculator.")
            break

        # Split input into components
        parts = user_input.split()

        # Check if the input is valid
        try:
            if len(parts) != 3:
                raise FormulaError("Formula must consist of
3 elements: number operator number.")

            # Attempt to convert the first and third inputs
to float
            num1 = float(parts[0])
            num2 = float(parts[2])

            # Check if the operator is valid
            operator = parts[1]
            if operator not in ['+', '-']:
                raise FormulaError("Operator must be '+' or
'-'.")
```

```
            # Perform the calculation based on the operator
            if operator == '+':
                result = num1 + num2
            elif operator == '-':
                result = num1 - num2

            print(f"Result: {result}")

        except ValueError:
            raise FormulaError("Invalid number format. Please enter valid numbers.")
        except FormulaError as e:
            print(f"Formula Error: {e}")

# Call the function to start the interactive calculator
calculate()
```

**CO5: Apply Python frameworks like NumPy and Pandas (All).**

21. **Write a Python program to create a numpy array of given shape and perform basic mathematical operations.**

**Ans 21:** import numpy as np

```
# Function to create a numpy array of a given shape
def create_and_operate_array(shape):
    # Create a numpy array of given shape with random integers
    arr = np.random.randint(1, 10, size=shape)  # Random integers between 1 and 10

    print(f"Original Array (Shape: {shape}):\n{arr}")

    # Perform basic mathematical operations
    addition = arr + 5  # Adding 5 to each element
    subtraction = arr - 3  # Subtracting 3 from each element
    multiplication = arr * 2  # Multiplying each element by 2
    division = arr / 2  # Dividing each element by 2 (floating point result)
```

```
    # Display the results of mathematical operations
    print("\nAfter Addition (arr + 5):\n", addition)
    print("\nAfter Subtraction (arr - 3):\n", subtraction)
    print("\nAfter Multiplication (arr * 2):\n", multiplication)
    print("\nAfter Division (arr / 2):\n", division)


# Example: Create a numpy array with shape (3, 3)
shape = (3, 3)  # A 3×3 array
create_and_operate_array(shape)
```

**22. Write a Python program to perform group by and aggregation on a Pandas data frame.**

**Ans 22:** import pandas as pd

```
# Sample DataFrame
data = {
        'Department': ['HR', 'Finance', 'HR', 'Finance',
'Engineering', 'Engineering', 'HR'],
      'Employee': ['John', 'Alice', 'Bob', 'David', 'Eve',
'Frank', 'Grace'],
      'Salary': [50000, 70000, 55000, 75000, 80000, 85000,
60000],
    'Age': [28, 34, 25, 45, 30, 38, 29]
}


# Create a DataFrame
df = pd.DataFrame(data)


# Perform groupby on the 'Department' column and apply
aggregation
grouped = df.groupby('Department').agg(
      total_salary=('Salary', 'sum'),    # Total salary by
department
     average_salary=('Salary', 'mean'), # Average salary by
department
     max_salary=('Salary', 'max'),      # Maximum salary by
department
```

```
employee_count=('Employee', 'count'), # Number of employees per department
    average_age=('Age', 'mean')        # Average age by department
)

# Display the result
print(grouped)
```

**CO6: Apply data visualization tools such as Matplotlib and Seaborn (All).**

**23. Create Box plot, Scatter Plot and Histogram with Matplotlib.**

**Ans 23:** import matplotlib.pyplot as plt

```
import numpy as np

# Generate random data for plotting
np.random.seed(0)
data = np.random.randn(1000)  # 1000 random numbers from a normal distribution
x = np.random.rand(100)  # 100 random numbers for the scatter plot
y = 2 * x + 1 + np.random.randn(100) * 0.2  # Linearly correlated data with noise for scatter plot

# 1. Box Plot
plt.figure(figsize=(8, 6))
plt.subplot(131)  # First subplot in a 1×3 grid
plt.boxplot(data)
plt.title("Box Plot")

# 2. Scatter Plot
plt.subplot(132)  # Second subplot in a 1×3 grid
plt.scatter(x, y, color='r', alpha=0.5)
plt.title("Scatter Plot")
plt.xlabel("X values")
plt.ylabel("Y values")
```

```
# 3. Histogram
plt.subplot(133)  # Third subplot in a 1×3 grid
plt.hist(data, bins=30, edgecolor='black')
plt.title("Histogram")
plt.xlabel("Value")
plt.ylabel("Frequency")

# Adjust layout for better
```

**24. Create Pair plot, Heatmap and Distribution plot with Seaborn.**

**Ans 24:** import seaborn as sns

```
import matplotlib.pyplot as plt
import numpy as np
import pandas as pd

# Generate random data for demonstration
np.random.seed(0)
data = {
    'A': np.random.randn(100),
    'B': np.random.randn(100),
    'C': np.random.randn(100),
    'D': np.random.randn(100)
}
df = pd.DataFrame(data)

# 1. Pair Plot
plt.figure(figsize=(8, 6))
sns.pairplot(df)
plt.suptitle("Pair Plot", y=1.02)
plt.show()

# 2. Heatmap
# Compute the correlation matrix
```

```
corr_matrix = df.corr()

plt.figure(figsize=(8, 6))
sns.heatmap(corr_matrix,    annot=True,    cmap='coolwarm',
linewidths=0.5)
plt.title("Heatmap of Correlation Matrix")
plt.show()

# 3. Distribution Plot
plt.figure(figsize=(8, 6))
sns.histplot(df['A'], kde=True, color='blue', bins=20)
plt.title("Distribution Plot for Column A")
plt.show()
```

9 789348 642899

Printed at Repro India Ltd.